THE CEELY ROSE
MURDERS
—— AT ——
MALABAR FARM

THE CEELY ROSE
MURDERS
— AT —
MALABAR FARM

MARK SEBASTIAN JORDAN

THE
History
PRESS

Published by The History Press
Charleston, SC
www.historypress.com

First published 2021

Manufactured in the United States

ISBN 9781467146180

Library of Congress Control Number: 2021934608

Notice: The information in this book is true and complete to the best of our knowledge. It is offered without guarantee on the part of the author or The History Press. The author and The History Press disclaim all liability in connection with the use of this book.

For all the friends, family and fans who have kept me going.

CONTENTS

PREFACE

I felt an odd mixture of familiarity and strangeness as I drove through Pleasant Valley. I had once spent a tremendous amount of my time there, directing play productions, working at Malabar Farm State Park and later operating a hostel on park grounds. Since I had left, not a lot had changed, although of course each minor difference seemed monumental, considering how intimately I once knew this place. The mighty maple in front of the old hostel had come down. The Malabar Farm Restaurant was closed for renovations. The ornate Big House mailbox had been taken down. This place was no longer home to me. I was there on a mission. I was returning to finish the book I'd been threatening to write for almost twenty years.

Pleasant Valley is a broad, beautiful valley running northwest–southeast in the lower-right corner of Richland County, Ohio. It was one of the first parts of the region to be settled. Its fame has circulated internationally on the basis of both the Ceely Rose case and the later appearance of Pulitzer Prize–winning American novelist and conservationist Louis Bromfield. Malabar Farm is Bromfield's estate, transformed into a public park after his death. In more recent years, the valley again became famous as the home of the Shawshank Oak, the massive tree featured in the classic film *The Shawshank Redemption*. It sat in the field next to Valley Hall School, the one-room schoolhouse Ceely Rose attended, until the tree fell.

The valley's significance in earlier times wasn't just as a gateway into Richland County. It was one of the last deep valleys of Appalachia;

indeed, the stone cliffs that stopped the advance of the last ice age twelve thousand years ago hang over both Bromfield's Big House mansion and the small Rose farmhouse. This place was the gateway by which humans returned to the ice-scoured ground made rich by deposits of soil as the glacier retreated. This was a borderland separating flat farmland from the hills of Appalachia—separating the townsfolk of the county seat, Mansfield, from the rural farmers. It was even in some sense a border separating North from South, for the hill settlers of Ohio tended to come from points farther south, often harboring sympathy for the Confederate cause during the Civil War (and still highly decorated with Confederate flags and bumper stickers today). The northern part of the state was settled by New Englanders and middle colony people. The Mason-Dixon line may have been a few hundred miles south, but culturally, this was the border. Holmes County, just a few miles southeast of Pleasant Valley, was home to an open armed rebellion, quickly crushed at "Fort Fizzle" in 1863. That same year, Copperhead Democratic presidential candidate Clement Vallandigham was arrested for treason by Lincoln's troops on the square in Mount Vernon, just a few miles due south. While most of the Pleasant Valley residents remained loyal to the Union, there was still a sense that they were apart from the county seat of Mansfield, an aspiring industrial city with a completely Northern feel.

The Rose family was from deep southern Ohio. Even among the country folk of Pleasant Valley, they were even more country. In sixteen years of residence, it seems they never entirely lost the identification as outsiders and strangers. Their own private family dysfunctions did nothing to diffuse that impression. I'm glad I waited to write this book. It took me years to understand how the Ceely Rose case wasn't merely the story of one family's self-destruction—it was the story of an entire society that had trouble figuring out what to do with an outsider. It's an issue we still have today. I wish I could say I were confident that we'd do a better job dealing with Celia Rose today. Often, I doubt we'd even do as well as the people of Pleasant Valley did 125 years ago.

I parked the car in front of the Pleasant Valley Lutheran Church, the same church where Celia Rose confessed to her friend that she had murdered her family. As I walked toward the Rose family graves in the cemetery across the road, I became aware of the peripheral names in the story, spread out around me: here were Ceely's defenders, the Ohlers; the neighbors, the Berrys; Flora Schrack, who wrote an eyewitness account; and even Guy Berry, the object of Ceely's obsession. In death, he lies only

The Pleasant Valley Cemetery was originally the graveyard for the Pleasant Valley Lutheran Church. *Author's collection.*

a dozen yards from the family whom Ceely Rose poisoned, thinking this would clear her path to her true love. Instead, Celia herself lies buried more than one hundred miles away in the patients' cemetery of the Lima State Hospital. The resonance of these stories was palpable.

My own involvement with this case goes back to 1982, when I was twelve years old. That Halloween, my mother, knowing my already well-developed taste for the macabre, pointed out an article in the newspaper. It was a typical Associated Press filler article, something originally created as a news release by the Ohio Department of Natural Resources, about alleged hauntings in state parks. I was surprised to find that the bulk of the article was devoted to a local legend, Ceely Rose, who had poisoned her entire family in 1896 in a small farmhouse still on the grounds of Malabar Farm State Park, where I had once gone on a school field trip. This fascinated me and became the motivation for future visits to the park, where I took tours and learned more about the case.

For a number of years, I forgot about Ceely Rose. I grew up and became very involved in regional theater as an actor, writer and director. In 1994, I was working in the office of a scrapyard run by my uncle (because theater in rural Ohio sure as hell won't pay the bills) when I took a lunch break and stopped by the bookstore in the nearby mall. I found a book titled *Haunted Ohio* by Chris Woodyard. Suffice it to say that little work got done that afternoon in the office when I discovered that the first section of the second chapter of her book was devoted to the Ceely Rose murders. Woodyard had plunged into the archives to consult some of the original media coverage of the case, bringing it to life in my mind's eye. I got chills not just because of the spooky story, but because I immediately knew that it was going to be my next play.

That summer, while working as an assistant stage manager on a production of *South Pacific* directed by Larry Evans at the Renaissance Theater in Mansfield, I plunged into research. I spent my free hours in the John Sherman History Room at the Mansfield/Richland County Public Library, pestering reference librarian Boyd Addlesperger for help with the cranky microfilm machines. My research assistant—my twelve-year-old niece Michelle—and I pored through old newspapers for hours on end, turning up tremendous amounts of long-forgotten information. I spent a lot of money ordering records from the National Archives and making trips to the places involved in the story. Wrapped up in these source materials, I wrote my first draft of the play in less than a week. I later revised the script and submitted it to a new play competition held by the Ohio Theatre Alliance, where it won an honorable mention.

Then, not knowing what to do with it and unable to find any Mansfield community theaters willing to produce a new full-length work, I sat on the script for a few years. My friend and theater technical director Daniel J. Feiertag insisted that the play had to be produced, so I finally contacted Malabar Farm State Park, asked if it could be presented there and found an eager collaborator in park manager Louis Andres. By doing it as a co-production between the Malabar Farm Foundation and the Mansfield Playhouse, with community support from the Richland County Foundation, we were able to finally bring Ceely to life in 2003. The first production—presented in the very barn at Malabar Farm that contains beams from the original gristmill that Ceely's father operated—sold out before it even opened. This led to a series of productions of *Ceely* and other historical dramas over the next dozen years.

All that time, I meant to start writing a book that would set down the historical details I had dug up over the years, without the compression and dramatic license necessary for a stage presentation. But it never felt right. It was only many years later, after I'd become more practiced in writing history and more attuned to the outward ripples of the story, that I was finally ready to write this story. After so much preparation, it seems a startlingly slim book to me. But I hope it will preserve knowledge of this infamous case and serve as a springboard to any future researchers who come along.

ACKNOWLEDGEMENTS

RESEARCH

James R. Bowsher, Jerry Pearson, Timothy Brian McKee, Brett Mitchell, James Dailey, Chris Woodyard, Michelle Jordan-Frias, Walt Bowsher, Boyd Addlesperger, Jayson Schlechty, Kenny Libben, Marie Herlevi, James Reed, Dr. Robert Berry, Joe and Pat Smith, Dr. Blake Wagner, Steve McQuown, Yolanda Campbell Lifter, Sherry Knight, Christine Rose, Chuck Salmons, Tyler A. Norris, Kelsey Denney, Mark Hersman, Dawn Shimp, Michelle Italia Walker, Julie Wittmer, Andrea Wittmer, Jim Stoner, Amie Lynn, Stephanie Bugg and Ginger Patterson.

PRODUCTION

Daniel J. Feiertag, Louis Andres, Steve and Debbie Kramer, Mary Ann Calhoun, Laura Callahan, Victoria Cochran, Dan and Sue Haeseker, Jim and Debbie Shade, Sybil Burskey and Lori Morey.

PROMOTIONAL

Ed Gutchall, Tommy Barnes, Rusty Cates, Chelley Kemper, Jodi Snavely, Lee Tasseff, Jamie Kinton, Norm Narvaja, Beth Santore, Brittany Schock, Grant Pepper, Linette Porter, Mike and Christina Petee, Eric and Judy Defibaugh, Paul Smith, Gina Jessee, Leigh Ann Arnholt, Becky Avery, Lori Morey, David Fitzsimmons, Wendy Zarara, Joshua Andra, Beth Donaldson, Keli Dotson, Deborah Dubois, Mary Frankenfield, Kinsey Landin, Danica Perry, Natasha Waltz, Emily Menshouse and Debbie Smith.

PERSONAL

Nancy Nixon, Jill and Andy Poloni, Bryan Gladden, Robin Greene, Annie Tarpley, Sharron Coeurvie, D'Aine Greene, Maysel Brooks, Jennifer Hurst, Jennifer Hunter, Will Cowman, Paige Nichol Jordan, Dr. Larry J. Evans, Steve Easterling, Llalan Fowler, Beth Wright-Archer, Chevy Bond, Victoria Hoefler, Tabitha Kennedy, Lucas Hargis, Amaliya Renock, Andy Nelson, Dan Hardwick, Brian Moore, Edward Lee Fox, Tommy Sarmiento and Lloyd and Violet Jordan.

INSTITUTIONS AND DATABASES

Akron/Stark County Public Library; Cleo Redd Fisher Museum/Mohican Historical Society; Division of Forestry, Ohio Department of Natural Resources (ODNR); Division of Geological Survey, ODNR; John Sherman Room, Mansfield, Richland County Public Library; Lima State Hospital; Madison County Probate Court; Malabar Farm Foundation; Malabar Farm State Park; The Mansfield Playhouse; Mansfield Reformatory Preservation Society; Oakwood Correctional Institution; Ohio Department of Corrections; Ohio Genealogical Society; Ohio History Connection; The Ohio State University, Mansfield; Ohio Theatre Alliance; Richland County Foundation; Richland County Probate Court; Rootsweb.com; and Rose Family Association.

MYSTERIOUS DEATHS

As spring turned to summer that year in Pleasant Valley, the weather had been off. The rains of the spring of 1896 hadn't ended as June tried to ripen into summer. Good weather for potato bugs and other pests. Bad weather for planting. Bad weather for milling.

Half deaf from ending up too close to the fighting decades before in the Civil War, David Rose could work only intermittently throughout the year at the old Schrack Mill. David had bought the shambling hulk when he moved his family north from southern Ohio into the highlands of Richland County, near Lucas, in 1879. In an age when old water-powered mills were rapidly being replaced by gasoline-powered threshers, Rose was able to buy the three-story mill for a song, although limited business kept his income fitful.

Rebecca, his wife, helped support the family by weaving rugs in the front parlor of the small two-story miller's house that sat across Switzer's Run from the mill. If David was known for being irascible, Rebecca was known as the rock of the family—determined, immovable.

Their son Walter was almost forty but still living at home. Walter alternated between working as a day laborer for neighboring farmers and helping his father at the mill when David's shaky health limited him. He also tended the pigs the family raised for food.

Then there was Ceely. Her given name was "Celia" but pronounced with a long *e* sound, as befits the Appalachian foothills of Pike County,

Pleasant Valley. Valley Hall School is at far left, Herring farm is at near center, Berry farm and former site of Schrack Mill are at mid center and the miller's house is at far right. *Ohio Department of Natural Resources/Malabar Farm State Park.*

Ohio, where she was born in 1873. Even after sixteen years in north-central Ohio, the Roses were still regarded as the outsiders, a bit coarser than the rest of the rural community.

Ceely Rose was well known around the valley as even more of an outsider. Shy and giggly, she was referred to as a girl, even though she was, in fact, twenty-three years old. She was thought to be a little slow by those who dealt with her, earning her the nickname "Silly Rose." For years she had attended the one-room red brick Valley Hall School, without ever progressing much further than the most basic skills. At recess, she could be found either playing with the little children or cheering the boys as they played ball.

At home, Ceely had been taught the simpler skills of housekeeping, including some cooking and sewing, but she showed little ability for anything as complicated as weaving.

Celia seemed, at best, a simpleton to be tolerated—at worst, an imbecile to be ignored. She seemed otherwise harmless to everyone she knew.

They could not have been more wrong.

ON TUESDAY, JUNE 23, David Rose was feeling strong enough to get some work done. He walked upstream from the mill to the two millponds and opened the sluice gates to fill them. By tomorrow, he'd be able to release the water to run down the sluice, gradually angling along the riverbank to enter the basement of the mill and turn the waterwheel. The exertion tired him, but he slept well that night.

Breakfast Wednesday morning, June 24, was eggs, slices of bread, bowls of cottage cheese with cherries from a tin can and coffee. Some accounts claim that Ceely made all of it; others state that she merely helped her mother, preparing certain parts of it. David was hungry and ate two full plates. Walter ate a full plate, while Rebecca had only a little, due to the headache with which she had awoken.

David noticed that Ceely was standing by, watching them, not eating. He asked her if she was going to fix a plate for herself. The girl seemed startled by the question, but she then picked up a plate and spooned a small amount of the eggs and cottage cheese on the plate. She didn't touch it.

Finished with breakfast, everyone prepared to get to work. David headed to the mill to get started on the large feed grinding order he had set up the day before. Walter put on his jacket and headed up Ferguson way with a gallon pail to investigate a rumor of some black raspberries having already ripened along the edge of the woods. Rebecca prepared to start a new rug on her loom.

Before setting up the loom, Rebecca noticed that she had come down with a terrible thirst. She asked Ceely to fetch her a cup of water. Ceely did so. When Rebecca took a deep drink, her stomach muscles suddenly convulsed, causing her to vomit so violently that she collapsed on the kitchen floor. The explosive action made Ceely giggle.

Rebecca tried to rise up, but further convulsions returned her to the floor. She could not stop vomiting. She ordered the girl to go get her father at the mill. Ceely ran out into the yard, avoiding the foul-tempered chickens that often pecked at her legs, crossed the rickety bridge over Switzer's Run and alerted David that Rebecca was "puking all over the place."

David hurried back to the house and helped Rebecca into a chair, where she continued to suffer stomach pains, even though her stomach had emptied its contents. When she attempted to down more water to combat her intense thirst, it again came back up. David realized that her illness was serious and headed outside to hitch up the horse and buggy. He knew that their usual family doctor, Dr. Budd of Perrysville, was out of town that week, so he headed south over the ridge toward Newville, where a younger doctor had recently set up shop.

By the time David Rose arrived at Dr. John McCombs's residence in Newville, his mouth had dried out severely. He explained his wife's illness to the doctor, who immediately readied himself to accompany Rose back to

Newville, where first responder Dr. John McCombs was called on by David Rose to tend his ill family. *John Sherman Room at the Mansfield/Richland County Public Library.*

the mill house. As they rushed back up onto the ridge, David's sense of thirst became maddeningly keen. He begged off to stop at a farmhouse and ask for some water. It isn't known which farm they stopped at, although it could have been at the Ferguson farm on Newville Road, but the result of David drinking water was instant and violent. He collapsed into severe stomach convulsions and vomiting. The doctor succeeded in loading David back into the buggy and sped on over the ridge into Pleasant Valley. With some effort, and some help from Ceely, he was able to get David back into the cottage and into the front parlor, where he lowered the old man onto a couch.

While this was going on, a neighbor suddenly pounded on the front door with an emergency: he had just found Walter Rose up the road by the Ferguson Woods, passed out in the ditch. He had thrown up. He must have come out and collapsed just moments after the doctor passed through with his father, unless in his haste the doctor had sped past and never even noticed Walter fallen near the road. The doctor went and gathered up Walter, returning him to the house and attempting to make him comfortable on a cot in the back parlor. Dr. McCombs looked around at the sick and moaning family, violently ill…except for one.

Ceely Rose stood to the side, wide-eyed, watching it all with fascination.

A DREAM HALTED

The Rose family was part of a general exodus of close-knit clans from Schoharie and Rensselaer Counties in upstate New York to the southern Ohio frontier in the early 1800s. Avoiding the quickly growing communities such as Columbus and Cincinnati, these families sought the rural hills of Highland and surrounding counties such as Brown, Adams, Pike and Ross—areas not unlike upstate New York and not unlike the ancestral homes of some of the families in the hilly northern parts of Hesse in central Germany.

With the rugged, unglaciated hills of southern Ohio came swift-flowing streams, an ideal site for milling. Lawrence Rose came to the area shortly after the death of his grandfather Wilhelm Roos in Colchester, New York, in 1819. DNA testing has proven that relationship, although it is unknown which of Roos's sons was Lawrence's father. What is known is that Lawrence Rose took on the trade of milling in Highland County, and he trained his son David, born on June 2, 1829, to be a miller too.

Lawrence's wife was Thankful Reynolds, daughter of Daniel Reynolds and Lucretia Worden, from families of English descent also living in Rensselaer County, New York. Lawrence and Thankful married in Brown County, Ohio, in 1820 and soon set up house at a mill somewhere in Highland County, most likely in the eastern part of the county, near the village of Sinking Spring, which straddles the border between Highland and Pike.

When David Rose later married, he wed a young woman from the Easter family. The Easters appear to have come through Pennsylvania and trace

Sinking Spring, on the border of Highland and Pike Counties, was central to the area where the Rose family lived in the early to mid-1800s. *Author's collection.*

back to the Öster surname of Germany. Jacob Easter came to Highland County as a young man, marrying Margaret Stultz in 1825. Their daughter Rebecca was born on August 23, 1834.

Little is known of David and Rebecca's early years, including when they first met. They were married by Justice of the Peace James Hetherington in Concord Township on February 8, 1855. The surviving tintype photographs of the two appear to have been from an engagement or wedding locket later given to their surviving daughter.

How long David Smith Rose apprenticed with his father, or if he even did, is uncertain, although it must be thought probable, as David appears in the 1850 census living with his parents in Brush Creek Township in southeast Highland County. Both David and his father are listed as millers.

Their mill may have been on Brush Creek or one of its tributaries. The creek flows southward out of the county into Adams County, passing beneath the bluff where the prehistoric Serpent Mound effigy earthwork is perched, before the creek joins the Scioto River, which soon exits into the vast Ohio River. The entire area of Brush Creek Township is the center of an ancient meteorite impact crater that shattered bedrock throughout an eight-mile-wide circle.

David S. Rose and his fiancée, Rebecca Easter, in about 1854. *James R. Bowsher Collection.*

When the time came for David to set up his own homestead, it had to be near a mill, where he could pursue his trade. This apparently took him farther into the region's rough hills, into Pike County, east of Sinking Spring. Early histories of the county do not record a great deal of information about mills, so it is impossible to know whether Rose had a mill of his own. In all likelihood he did not, as his property does not directly touch on the nearest body of water, Shoemaker Creek, which is more of a stream than a creek anyway. He may, however, have rented someone else's mill or worked in a mill owned and supervised by someone else. There was a mill near Byington, on Sunfish Creek, run by a number of different owners throughout the nineteenth century, but David Rose is not listed among them. If he worked there as an assistant, it would be a longish daily commute by horse. More likely, he worked at the mill at Kincaid Springs, near the village of Latham, within reasonable walking distance.

In 1854, David went in with his brother-in-law, Philip Rhoads, to purchase a parcel of land just north of Latham in Pike County's Mifflin Township, just seven miles east of Sinking Spring. The land straddles a modest ridge between Campbell Hill and Latham Hill. Atop the six-hundred-foot-tall ridge were unimproved forests, perhaps including some of the poplar trees sought after for lumber in this area in the mid-nineteenth century. If so, then Rose's aim may have been to not only build and farm on the property but also to lumber it. That latter activity would have been curtailed by his

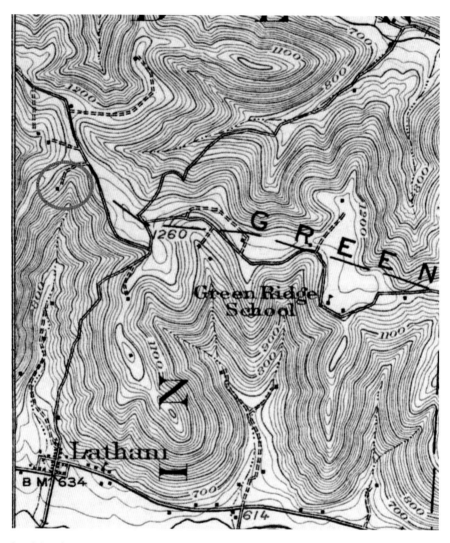

health after the war. Some cropping may have been possible on cleared land, but the soil is thin on the ridge, so it is likely phosphate fertilizer would have been necessary for any extensive raising of crops. It would be more likely that, like many farm families in Appalachia, the Roses kept a vegetable garden for their own needs and left the rest of the cleared land as grazing pastures for livestock. Indeed, the 1860 Pike County farm census identifies Rose as having eighty acres, only seven acres of which are improved. The family was in possession of one horse, one milch cow and five hogs. No farm equipment was noted, and the only cropping done was sixty bushels of Indian corn, presumably raised as hog feed. In 1865,

Opposite: This topographic map of Pike County shows the location of the now abandoned Rose farm, 1854–79. *U.S. Geological Survey.*

Above: The farmhouse and workable land were in a narrow seven-acre strip atop this ridge, while the rest of the property sloped away steeply. *Author's collection.*

Rose bought out his brother-in-law's portion of the land and just a month later sold the southern half of the property to David Kniesley. That left the Roses living on a sixty-three-acre parcel.

The land today is part of the Pike National Forest. Although no structures survive on the property, the 1915 U.S. Geological Survey topographical map indicates a building standing near the northeast corner of the property, on the top of the ridge. Inspection of the site supports the idea that this would have been the location of the house or cabin for the farm, as the top of the ridge is the only ground anywhere close to level on the entire property. The hill's sides slope away at a precipitous angle unsuitable for building. What's more is that the general ridgetop area matches up very conveniently to the seven-acre improved part of the land described in the 1860 farm census. A potential house foundation is visible about where the structure was indicated on the topographical map. A spring lies just a quarter mile south on the top of the ridge.

David and Rebecca's married life did not start easily. In 1856, Rebecca gave birth to a son they named John. Unfortunately, the rate of infant mortality in nineteenth-century Ohio was high, particularly in a rural backcountry area. John did not survive a year. On December 1, 1857, their second son, Walter W., was born. Although later descriptions of him did not compliment his intelligence or manner, he was strong enough to survive. At some point in 1859, a daughter, Julia Ann, was born to the Roses. It looked like they might finally flourish as a family.

That dream was halted by the outbreak of the Civil War. David patriotically enlisted on September 8, 1861, offering his skills as a miller to the army. Assigned to the Sixty-Third Ohio Volunteer Infantry, Rose plied his trade in the service of a frequently relocating regiment. But it shouldn't be thought that he was safe from the fighting by working as a miller, for the rapidly changing shape of a battle all but guaranteed that non-fighters would also get swept up in the action at times.

Under Colonel John W. Sprague, the Sixty-Third OVI was put into the Ohio Brigade, which earned the surrender of Island No. 10 in the Mississippi River at New Madrid, Missouri, in early April 1862, allowing Union forces to pierce deep into the Confederacy. Later in the year, the regiment fought at the Battle of Iuka and in the Siege of Corinth. The year 1863 saw the regiment moving throughout northern Alabama. After an 1864 furlough allowed the men to return home for a visit to their families, the Sixty-Third OVI became part of General William T. Sherman's Atlanta Campaign and then was included in the following March to the Sea. After some mop-up work in the Carolinas, the regiment was part of the Grand Review of the Armies in May 1865. The regiment was mustered out on July 8, 1865, in Louisville, Kentucky.

Where was David Rose in all this? He was probably not there at all for many of the later activities. We don't know the details, but Rose's surviving military service record in the National Archives tells the story of a rocky career at best. At a Special Muster on August 18, 1862, Rose was marked down as "Deserted July 23 '62. Supposed to be in Highland Co. O." One wonders if he returned home to help Rebecca and the children. He may also have been concerned about the declining health of his father. Lawrence Rose finally passed away on June 15, 1864, and was buried at the Olive Branch Cemetery, west of Sinking Spring.

At some point, David returned to duty, but it wasn't his last unexcused absence. On April 17, 1863, Rose deserted, only to return on April 30. On October 31, in Memphis, Tennessee, he was listed as "Sick in

David Rose in a later illustration, apparently based on a photograph that has not survived. *James Reed Collection.*

quarters." He was sick at Decatur, Alabama, on May 1, 1864, and was admitted into the General Hospital in Chattanooga, Tennessee, because of "chronic diarrhea" on May 17. Evidently, his case was so severe that he was transferred to the No. 1 General Hospital in Nashville two days later. On May 22, he was transferred to a hospital steamboat, the USS *Chas. McDougal*, which transported him to the No. 6 General Hospital in New Albany, Maryland, where he was admitted four days later. He finally returned to the regiment on June 30, 1864. He was furloughed on August

3, to visit home, but then deserted again on November 30 and never returned. Regardless, Rose was honorably discharged in January 1865.

When David Rose applied for disability in 1890, his stomach problems were cited, along with related disease of kidney and rectum, causing burning sensations and frequent urination at night. But the veteran's problems didn't end there. He also noted partial deafness in both ears resulting from his military service, suggesting that somewhere in the war, Rose may have been in proximity to weapon fire in battle. One form also claims "loss of right eye" as part of his disability.

Dr. Allen W. Budd of Perrysville, Ohio, swore an affidavit about having treated Rose for years for his chronic diarrhea. He also noted the eye issue: "Said claimant has but one eye. [The bad eye] is defective from past inflammatory trouble. I have known him to be confined to [a] dark room for days because of inflammation of eye."

The doctor then testified about Rose's hearing: "From past and present examination, I find almost complete deafness of right ear, with partial deafness of left ear. Partial loss of hearing has been continuous since my acquaintance with claimant. This I know from contact in his home and at my office." Budd summarized his professional opinion by saying, "The claimant shows marked evidence of General Debility."

Rose's fellow veteran Benjamin Elliott testified to the miller's continuing battle with stomach ailments after the war in a general affidavit filed in support of David's application for a disability pension: "I was a member of the same organization as claimant[,] Co. E. 63rd Reg. O.V.I. I knew that claimant had the army diarrhea very badly while in the service and I saw him immediately after his return home in 1865 and he was then very bad with diarrhea and did not work any for a considerable length of time after his return from the army on account of it. He still continued to be a great sufferer from this disease as long as he remained in this County which I think was about 1879. I know this to be a fact because I lived a neighbor to him within 1½ miles of him." This affidavit was filled out in response to a request delivered in his name to the Latham Post Office, suggesting that Rose did not keep in touch with the people from Pike County who were once his friends and neighbors. "[I] don't know any thing about his health at this time," Elliott added. Benjamin Elliott is buried at the Lapperell Cemetery, just a mile or so west of where Rose's property was. Neighbor Joseph Decker, who only lived a quarter mile away and saw Rose twice a week, sometimes working with and for him, also backed up Rose's claim.

The official examination of David Rose was conducted in Mansfield, Ohio, on March 18, 1891, by Drs. Patterson, Loughridge and Mitchell. They measured Rose's height at five feet, ten and one quarter inches; his weight at 169 pounds; pulse 104; respiration 20; and temperature 98.5 degrees. They noted his "[g]eneral appearance of less than ordinary health." They noted he could hear only words that are quite loudly spoken and that his right eye was entirely destroyed. The doctors recommended a partial disability pension, covering six out of the eighteen points worthy of disability rating. This gave David S. Rose a monthly pension payment of twelve dollars.

Clearly the war wreaked havoc on David Rose's health, as it did to many survivors. The Ohio Sixty-Third OVI lost 2 officers and 91 enlisted men in battle during the war but lost 5 officers and 259 enlisted men to disease.

If David's reunion with Rebecca was a joyous occasion, we have no evidence of it. While many families added a baby less than a year after a soldier's return, no records survive to indicate David and Rebecca had any more children.

That changed in 1873.

A FAMILY IN FLIGHT

Celia Frances Rose was born on March 13, 1873, in Pike County, eight years after her father David's return from the Civil War and a full fourteen years after her parents' previous child, Julia. This startling fact begs many questions: Had David and Rebecca kept trying to have children but lost several to miscarriage or infant mortality? Had they elected to practice some form of contraception, only to find it fail after their previous children were already nearly grown? Or was it something more sinister? While she would have been very young, it is not impossible that Julia Ann Rose could actually have been Celia's mother, with the grandparents electing to pose as parents to raise their child's child. This hypothetical scenario could mean either that the girl was impregnated by someone in the community or even as a result of an incestuous situation. Many have speculated, but at this late date, proof seems unlikely to arise.

If it is possible that a girl of fourteen in the 1870s had already experienced menarche, it is also equally possible that Rebecca Rose had not yet entered menopause at the age of thirty-nine, although many women did enter it by age forty in the nineteenth century. It could be the case that Rebecca thought she was far enough along in perimenopause to stop making use of contraception, opening her up to an accidental pregnancy, a "change-of-life baby," as such advanced cases were called in that era.

We know nothing of Celia Rose's childhood except that while her first name was always spelled that way, it seems always to have been pronounced "Ceely," the form her legend has preserved. This is typical of the older English pronunciation styles that remained in use in more remote regions of the growing United States, surviving in Appalachia until the twentieth century. Highland and Pike Counties are officially classified as part of Appalachia by the Appalachian Regional Commission, and Richland County, where they later moved, stands just a few miles away from the political border of Appalachia in that part of Ohio.

We know from the 1870 census that Walter and Julia Ann were attending school, either in the nearby school in Latham or in the rural school farther up the road their farmhouse lay closest to. But that census also notes that the two children could read but not write, so their schooling was probably limited. Beyond that, information is scarce. By the 1880 census, the Rose family had relocated to southern Richland County, Ohio, in the north-central part of the state, a good 150 miles away from Latham. There is nothing to indicate the Roses had any relatives or friends where they ended up. Why did they flee southern Ohio?

The answer may never be known, but one wonders if it had something to do with Julia Ann Rose, for by the 1880 census, she has disappeared from all records. What happened to her is only partially known. There is a record in the Pike County Probate Court that states that on November 15, 1876, Annie Rose married a John H. Long. John, born in 1858, was the son of James Long, a late Civil War casualty who died in the Gothic Hospital in Paducah, Kentucky, in 1866. His mother, Mary (neé Redding), remarried to a man named James Gault (sometimes rendered "Gott" on census reports).

By the census of 1880, Julia Ann (or Annie) Long is nowhere to be found. We know from much later on, however, that when Rebecca Rose was murdered, the will composed on her death bed cited a grandson named John Long. That supports the assumption that "Annie Long" is the same person as Julia Ann Long. While the older John H. Long is elusive in the 1880 census, a young John H. Long shows up at the age of two, living with the family of George Long, the boy's uncle, in Perry Township of Ross County, just a short distance north of where the Roses lived.

Perusal of earlier census reports shows that John H. Long Sr. had a younger brother named George. Furthermore, the 1880 Ross County census shows that Mary Gott (Gault) was living with George's family, her second husband, James Gault, having died in 1877. Wherever he was in 1880, John H. Long Sr. later ends up living in Greene County, near the town of Xenia, with his new wife, Marie.

Tying all this information together, the spotty trail of records hints at a tragic story: Julia Ann Rose marries John H. Long on November 15, 1876.

In December, David and Rebecca sell a sixty-three-acre property to John H. Long for $600. Just six months later, he sells it back, although the deed now lists only Rebecca Rose, for $700. Was there a falling out between the families that made John Long want to distance himself from the Roses? Did he run into severe financial problems and the Roses rescued him by buying back the land he and Julia Ann were possibly already living on? Or did they have to leave the county to pursue a work opportunity?

Somewhere between here and the following year, a son was born, named after his father. But no period document proves the date of the boy's birth. Later family records place it in 1878, which would be after the mysterious land transaction. But the birth could have been earlier. At any rate, Julia Ann either died in childbirth or within two years of it, for by 1880, the little boy is living with his uncle, George Long, and his grandmother Mary Gault. The father appears to have passed the boy on to relatives so he could find a new wife and start a new life.

No death record or cemetery record exists for Julia Ann, but that's not uncommon for this area and period. Although there was a state law in Ohio instructing counties to keep death records, it was a mandate that was not funded and enforced until 1908. One can easily imagine a death going unrecorded in western Pike County, considering that the county seat lay well to the eastern end of the county, over rough terrain. And if Julia Ann Long were buried at a country cemetery with only a fieldstone to mark her final resting place, she would merely be one among thousands lying forgotten in Appalachian hillside cemeteries. Her disappearance remains a mystery.

The timing of Julia Ann's death and the Rose family's departure for the opposite end of the state may be coincidental, or it might not be. It certainly isn't hard to imagine the family wanting to put distance between themselves and a tragic loss of a loved one. Rebecca sold the land in November 1879, and later affidavits by neighbors cite 1879 as the date that the Roses left Pike County.

It is very interesting that the Roses did not end up with little John H. Long. Does this again hint at a falling out between the Roses and Longs? Was there some element of Julia's death that remained a sore point between the families? No surviving newspapers from Pike County offer any insight, although, again, they mainly carried news from the eastern end of the county and didn't have a lot to say about the western hills. To date, no diaries from the area have offered any insight either. What happened to Julia? It's unlikely we'll ever know.

The Schrack Mill, around 1879, when the Roses purchased it. The sluice run enters the building from the left. *Ohio Department of Natural Resources/Malabar Farm State Park.*

What is known is that in 1880, Rebecca Rose purchased the decrepit old Schrack Mill in Pleasant Valley, south of Lucas, Ohio, in southern Richland County, from Christian Welty for $500. The mill and the miller's house sat on two acres "plus 68 rods," near the intersection of Newville Road and Hastings Road, on the grounds of what is today Malabar Farm State Park.

THE SCHRACK MILL WAS built by the first white settlers of Pleasant Valley in southeast Richland County, David and Charles Schrack, around 1820. The brothers built a large brick house for David, which also served as an inn for travelers coming up the Wheeling–Sandusky stagecoach road. That building still stands today, housing the Malabar Farm Restaurant. It was located next to the Niman Spring, a gushing water source that was often visited in the early 1800s by the colorful frontier entrepreneur John Chapman, better known as "Johnny Appleseed." He often visited the spring and likely slept in Schrack's yard, as he was said to not much care for indoor accommodations.

Next the brothers built a wooden house for Charles that doubled as a general store for the valley in its early years. They decided that directly behind Charles's house, they would erect a gristmill, and about a quarter of a mile down Switzer's Run (pronounced "swite-tser," reflecting the brothers' Swiss roots), they would build a sawmill. A quarter mile up the creek, around what is now the main entrance into Malabar Farm State Park, they built two impound ponds. Water was diverted from the creek into the ponds. Gates could then release water from the ponds to run down a wooden sluice that gradually angled downhill as it traveled along the bank of the creek, building up water pressure. Since this was a low valley and there was no waterfall, the Schrack Mill would never have employed a traditional sidewheel. Instead, the brothers built a breast wheel in the basement of the three-story structure, a large horizontal waterwheel. The sluice run entered the west side of the mill, turning the basement breast wheel, which turned the grindstones.

The Schracks obviously knew their milling and were determined to do it right. Instead of making do with local rock, David Schrack traveled to Philadelphia as the mills were being planned and ordered French buhrstones, to be shipped to Philadelphia and picked up the following year. The brothers built the mills in the intervening year. Dr. Joe Hannibal, the curator of invertebrate paleontology at the Cleveland Museum of Natural History,

The Malabar Farm Restaurant underwent restoration during the 2020 pandemic. *Author's collection.*

has examined surviving pieces of the buhrstones and noted that while the stones lack the miniscule fossils that would prove conclusively that they were quarried in the Marne Valley of France, in every other particular, they are consistent with such an origin.

Other accounts of the early years of the valley claimed that the buhrstones were Italian rock used as ballast in ships, although that wouldn't explain why Schrack would have to return east after a year to collect them. The French story, and Dr. Hannibal's study of the stones, makes the former explanation sound more plausible.

Unlike the large, single-piece grindstones popular in early mills, these wheels were made of chunks of rock that were banded together to make the millstone. That way, if one portion of the wheel sustained more wear than another, the entire millstone didn't have to be replaced, just one chunk. This also made it easier to sharpen the stones periodically. One of the sectional millstones survives, buried in the ground at the mill site. The other one has been taken apart and pieces lost over the years, although the steel banding remains near the original building foundation.

While it appears that the mill was still functional by 1879, it was likely nowhere near its prime. By this period, steam and gasoline-powered threshers were beginning to replace water-powered mills, and the Schrack Mill is unlikely to have received a huge amount of business. The selling price confirms it.

So, how did David S. Rose hear about a broken-down old mill available for cheap 150 miles away from where he lived? Was he connected with a network of professional millers who might have spread the word? Was he alerted to it by a former army comrade? The Ohio Sixty-Third OVI had been formed from southern Ohioans, but the gradual diaspora northward from Appalachia to the industrial Midwest had already begun trickling by the 1870s, so it's possible (though not particularly likely) that David Rose kept in touch with army buddies who later moved north. The ones who testified on his behalf regarding his disability pension said that they hadn't spoken to him since he left Pike County a decade earlier. Could there have been professionals who worked on mills that carried the news from northern to southern Ohio? Newspaper reports? We simply don't know.

David and Rebecca moved north around November 1879, taking Walter and Celia with them. The 1880 census does not show Julia Ann (Rose) Long with them or with family in southern Ohio. She was gone. Later paperwork from Madison County regarding the legal guardianship of John H. Long Jr. confirms that Julia died, although it does not name the date. It

Top: An original buhrstone section found near the site of the mill. *Bottom*: Dr. Joe Hannibal of the Cleveland Museum of Natural History examines the buhrstone. *Author's collection.*

does, however, describe John Long Sr. and Julia as being "late of Madison County." Perhaps this suggests that a job opportunity took John Long north to Madison County. If this is so, and if the boy was raised in Ross County by John's relatives, it may be that David and Rebecca Rose never even had the chance to meet their grandson, which might help explain their ability to depart the region and leave him behind.

The rest of the Rose and Easter clans remained in southern Ohio. No correspondence survives to indicate any close degree of connection between David and Rebecca and their kinfolk. Whether they ever saw their families again face to face is unknown.

OUTSIDERS IN THE VALLEY

When the Rose family moved to Pleasant Valley, centrally located in southeast Richland County, Ohio, between the villages of Lucas, Butler, Perrysville and Newville, not much had changed there in the decades since early settlement. Descendants of David Schrack still lived in the old stagecoach inn by the Niman Spring. Charles Schrack's home had been sold to the Berry family, but sometime well before that— even before the Civil War, apparently—the mill had been sold off and a small two-story house had been built for the miller's family.

A one-room schoolhouse, Valley Hall School, was built at the intersection of Hastings Road and Pleasant Valley Road. A rotating cast of teachers came through to educate the children of the valley, few staying longer than a year or two.

The Ferguson family lived up on the ridge overlooking the valley on the way to Newville, a village later obliterated by the formation of Pleasant Hill Reservoir. A farmer named Clem Herring lived with his mother, Phebe, just a quarter of a mile farther up Hastings Road from the miller's house. The Davis family lived on up the winding road from the Herrings.

Up Pleasant Valley Road (the former stagecoach route), heading toward the village of Little Washington, sat the gasworks where, as early as the 1870s, natural gas was being tapped and collected. It is still in operation today. Just beyond that is the Pleasant Valley Lutheran Church and its graveyard, attended by most residents of the valley in those days.

The David Schrack home—which later became the Malabar Farm Restaurant—was built around 1820 and doubled as a stagecoach inn. *Ohio Department of Natural Resources/Malabar Farm State Park.*

The next farm north of the church was the Ohler farm, which will come into the story later. Just before the Ohlers' is an outcropping in the valley wall known as Pipe's Cliff. The early Native American leader Hopocan, known to the settlers as Captain Pipe, used to visit this bluff every year until the 1830s. On each visit, even in extreme old age, he would climb the cliff and sit and pray to honor the memory of his sister Onolaska, who plummeted to her death from the bluff many years earlier when she was pursued by a patrol of British soldiers before the Revolutionary War. Even in the 1880s, there were still a handful of residents of the valley with memories of the stately Leni-Lenape chieftain. The past lingers in Pleasant Valley.

One of the first deep valleys to drain cool air from the western plains of Ohio, Pleasant Valley is one of the coldest spots in Ohio on sharp winter mornings. At times like that, the place seems to hold a memory of its origins twelve thousand years ago, carved by the retreating Wisconsin glacier, the final ice age sculptor of the north-central Ohio landscape. The cliffs that

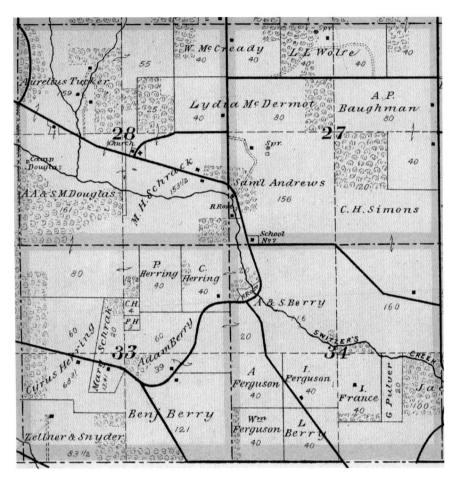

This plat map shows the locations of structures near the mill, although it mistakenly shows the miller's house and mill on the northern section, where the millponds were. *Timothy Brian McKee Collection.*

halted the glacier's last advance loom over the valley, shading the miller's cottage from the rising sun until midmorning.

The miller's house stands on a curve of Hastings Road (today Bromfield Road) where the old Newville Road (now used only as a state park access road) intersects. Switzer's Run cuts between the cottage and the site of the mill, now overgrown. The house today is different from the way it was laid out 150 years ago. Built some time before the Civil War, the house was a small, square, two-story farmhouse. Inside, the first floor was separated into a front parlor (in the southeast corner), a back parlor (on the northern side of the structure) and a kitchen, all small. A ladder provided the only access to the sleeping rooms on the top floor, and stairs led down to the cellar. The front porch was later lengthened by Louis Bromfield when he added a new, larger kitchen and a third upstairs room to the structure. Stairs were built to lead upstairs. Downstairs walls were demolished to make the original three tiny rooms into a single, modest-sized room. The original layout of rooms upstairs was changed to two bedrooms and a bathroom. Original rough plank doors remain. Even today, the rooms are far from spacious. The smallness of the original rooms must have had the effect of a pressure cooker when there was tension among the residents.

In the west yard of the house stood a springhouse, covering a spring that bubbled up from the roots of a giant elm tree later described by Louis Bromfield as one of the largest trees in the valley. The tree is discernable in a 1938 photo of the valley, although the springhouse is not. The spring fed a pond that was filled in by the State of Ohio when it took over the property to make it into a state park in 1972, according to Malabar Farm staff worker Joe Smith, who lived in the house in the late 1960s and early '70s until the state took over. By that time, the springhouse and elm tree

The miller's house still stands today at Malabar Farm State Park, though altered in structure with added rooms. *Author's collection.*

The Berry family lived in the Charles Schrack House, which had doubled as a residence and general store in its early days. *Ohio Department of Natural Resources/Malabar Farm State Park.*

were long gone. The spring, however, isn't entirely dead, even to this day. The house's west yard is often soaked.

Somewhere on this small parcel of land, the Roses kept hogs and raised both a vegetable garden and an herb garden. A small footbridge gave access over the creek to the Schrack Mill. Just above the mill, atop the hill, was the old Charles Schrack home, its front porch facing the intersection and the bridge. A wagon road passed in front of the big, two-story house and curved around the hill, entering the rear of the mill, where wagons could be loaded or unloaded and then continue out the other side of the building. Then they would pass along the sluice run and rejoin the road on the far side of the hill. By the time the Roses came to Pleasant Valley, George and Angeline Berry had moved into Charles Schrack's old house and started a family. What was now the Berry house and the miller's house were in direct sight of each other, only a few hundred feet apart, uncomfortably close by valley standards.

Rebecca Rose was the only one listed on the deed when the Roses purchased the mill and house from Christian Welty for $500 in July 1880. This may have been a strategy pursued to keep David's name off any property, for he immediately filed for a disability pension related to his army service as soon as they arrived at the mill. Considering the shape of

David Rose's health, it's surprising he undertook running the mill in the first place. The 1880 census report states that David was only employed about six months out of the year, although that may also reflect the lack of work available for an old mill.

One who may have helped David with whatever work was to be done was his son, Walter. At age twenty-three, when the family moved north, Walter is simply listed as a "laborer" on the 1880 census. Later recollections by neighbors said that Walter often worked as a day laborer, doing odd jobs for other farmers as needed. In this capacity, he may have helped his father at the mill as well. Oddly, though, Walter never displayed any inclination to leave the family home. In 1896, at age thirty-nine, he was still living there, still working as a day laborer.

Some have speculated about this. Was Walter that spectacularly unambitious? Or did he feel that his frail father would not be able to survive without assistance? While the youngest member of rural families often served as caretaker for aging parents, it may have seemed inescapable to Walter that young Ceely would herself need care for a lifetime, and with Julia gone and John Long Jr. living in southern Ohio, there was no one to care for them all but Walter himself. On the other hand, it seems strange that if that were the case, Walter didn't simply take over the day-to-day operations of the mill and let his father retire. But then again, the half-deaf miller had a reputation for being cranky. It may have been that there was no way for Walter to please his father one way or the other.

An in-depth story later run in the *Chicago Tribune* cited local opinion that if David Rose was known as not-to-be-crossed, Walter inherited an intensified version of his father's moods. The article described him as "fiery of temper, passionate and vindictive, though not dangerous." Although it dismissed him as being of less than average intelligence, it also described him as having a local reputation for being a shrewd huckster. No one ever got the best of Walter Rose in a deal.

There is no surviving evidence that Walter ever showed any interest in getting married and starting a family of his own. Was he a loner? Was he put off of the idea of having

Walter Rose. This photograph ran in a tabloid newspaper article in 1896. *James Reed Collection.*

a family because of the tragedy and dysfunction of his own family? Was he asexual? Homosexual? Unnaturally attached to Ceely? Could he even have been Ceely's real father? Many questions remain unanswered and unanswerable.

The family's meager living was helped by Rebecca, who worked the loom in the front parlor to weave rugs that she could sell for extra income. While the family was certainly not well off, it shouldn't be thought that they were borderline destitute either. The house was well stocked with the typical homely household items any farm family would have in the late nineteenth century (see the appendices). All of those items are known to have been in or around the house and mill. In many ways, the Roses were an average rural family, scrabbling together a decent though unspectacular living as best they could.

But then there was Ceely. By the time the Roses moved to Pleasant Valley, it would likely have been evident that Celia was "slow"—what we today would call developmentally disabled and what in the late 1800s was often termed as being an "imbecile" or "moron." Ceely was sent to Valley Hall School, but her progress was so fitful that she was not expected to attend daily. Her teachers later testified that Ceely stayed with the smaller children, even as she aged. Her teacher Minnie Andrews later opined that Ceely never got much above the mental level of a six-year-old and would play only with the first-year students, even when she was as old as twenty.

A later *Chicago Tribune* article vividly sketched Ceely's otherness: "Celia Rose from her childhood has been a puzzle to the simple, shrewd, practical country folk of this neighborhood. She would never work except when she was so inclined, no matter how busy or tired her mother might be. To children of her own age, she displayed an unsocial disposition, building her doll-houses in the woods on the bank of a Tennysonian brook. There she would stay for hours at a time, and no one cared to disturb her." The article goes on to say that anyone who tried to force the girl to do anything might end up with her teeth sunk in their arm.

As she grew through her teenage years and became even less social, Celia became notorious for silly, childish behavior, such as jumping out from behind doors to try to startle people. Once when she was visiting the Tucker family's house with her mother, Ceely became fascinated with the home's new wallpaper, which was printed with bright flowers. Ceely, already in her late teens by this time, crept from flower to flower, kissing

Valley Hall School, the one-room schoolhouse that Ceely Rose attended. Today, it is a private residence. *Author's collection.*

each one and giggling. The children of the valley nicknamed her "Silly Rose" for her antics.

On one occasion, Ceely was instructed to memorize a twenty-four-line verse for a Valley Hall School program. Eva Tucker said that Ceely was very nervous when she stood up in front of all the parents and began giggling uncontrollably. When she tried to speak the poem, she stammered too much to get it out. She finally had to take the paper the poem was printed on and hold it up to block her view of the audience. Then, finally, she was able to give the poem in its entirety, by reading it.

She was evidently an avid reader, having read and reread the books that the Roses owned, as well as reading every newspaper David brought home. But it was said that while she had a startling recall for a wide range of things she had read, her understanding of them was as limited as her own original ideas.

A stunning example of Celia Rose's limited grasp comes from a story that was shared by Elmer Cunning at her trial. Cunning was the teacher at Valley Hall School in the 1890–91 school year. One morning, it was raining extremely heavily, but all the students made it to school, save one. Cunning

Pipe's Cliff is a Pleasant Valley landmark connected in folklore with the native chief Captain Pipe. *John Sherman Room at the Mansfield/Richland County Public Library.*

presumed that Ceely was being kept home that day and that Rebecca Rose would send someone along presently to inform him. Cunning busied himself with the morning lessons.

When the classes paused for lunch, Mr. Cunning realized that Celia still hadn't shown up, yet there was no word from the Rose family about her absence. Cunning sent a student to run the quarter mile down the road to make sure all was well.

When the student got to the miller's house, Rebecca was startled to hear that Ceely wasn't at the schoolhouse. She had left that morning at the usual time. She and the student rushed back to the school. Cunning canceled classes for the rest of the day and began organizing search parties of nearby neighbors and some of the older students. One group headed farther down Pleasant Valley Road, most likely splitting to check the dirt road by the sawmill as well.

The other group headed up the valley, checking the farms, fields and woods as they went. They passed the Pleasant Valley Lutheran Church. They passed Pipe's Cliff. They passed the property where both the Tuckers and Ohlers lived. Somewhere miles up the stagecoach road, they spotted Ceely, soaked by the rain and dispiritedly trudging. As they ran up to her, she turned, and they saw that she was weeping bitterly. After they calmed her down, she haltingly spilled out the story of how she left for school in the heavy rain that morning, and she kept walking and walking but never got to school. The girl was tired, exhausted, confused and utterly soaked from the still-falling rain.

And so the stories pile up. Amanda Andrews overheard Ceely talking to herself like a small child playing make-believe might do. Phebe Herring said that Ceely at one point attempted to steal a book that had been delivered to her and her son's post box. Minnie Andrews opined that the girl was bright enough to know that certain things were crimes, for her mother often corrected her, but she was not bright enough to understand she shouldn't do them. Andrews went a step further and said that the balance of the family wasn't very bright and the parents weren't well educated. In an undated typewritten memoir by Angeline Schrack Heier in the archives at Malabar Farm, she noted that neither Ceely nor Walter had a high IQ and that "it was rumored that it was due to a close relationship between the parents."

Even as recently as the spring of 1896, Ceely had made a few isolated visits to the school, according to then-teacher Emma Halderman. On one occasion, she hadn't visited in a while and became convinced that the little girls wouldn't recognize her—she seemed delighted with the idea. She was perplexed, then, when the children all greeted her as usual.

Flora Schrack, Angeline's older sister, became a teacher and a professional writer. She penned her memories of the case many years later for the *Columbus Dispatch Magazine*. She, like other eyewitnesses to the case, is blunt: "Walter, a tall, awkward, somewhat dim-witted man of about 40, worked as a day laborer at odd jobs in the community. Celia, nicknamed 'Seely,' the Rose's [*sic*] retarded daughter, was a few years younger than Walter. A tall blonde with stringy hair stretched back into a large knot, she could perform only routine tasks about the house or garden."

At the time these events transpired, Flora was fifteen years old. Her sister Angeline was only nine. Yet Angeline's memories often come off as more accurate and more direct, although neither sister is perfect. Angeline apparently misremembered Rebecca Rose's name as "Peggy," when it was more likely shortened as "Becky." But she recalled that "Peggy" Rose and Angeline's grandmother were "the best of friends," suggesting that after a decade and half, the Roses weren't entirely outsiders. Angeline said that Mrs. Rose was kept so busy with her loom weaving carpet that Grandmother Schrack had to do the visiting, and she often brought young Angeline along with her to the miller's house, about a mile away. The girl enjoyed accompanying her grandmother, but she didn't want to stay inside the Roses' front parlor, where Rebecca had her loom set up.

"Now that loom was a noisy, clanging thing and I wanted to be outside," Angeline wrote. "The father, David, the miller, and always covered with flour, was back and forth many times daily between the house and the mill, and he and I became real pals. His frequent trips made a little path beside the stream, and I would follow him until finally he would give me a little piece of candy." She added that even though Switzer's Run was a shallow creek, she feared falling into it.

Like Flora, Angeline didn't have much complimentary to say about Walter. "The son Walter was sufficiently intelligent to work and make his own way, so he had what was then called a huckster wagon and he drove roundabout thru the neighborhood gathering up eggs from farmers for sale and delivering grocery staples to these farmers, thus saving them a trip to town. But this was another chance for me to get a piece of candy, and how eagerly I wanted for the day for the 'huckster' to come. And I never failed to get my little piece of striped candy."

Flora misremembered events as happening in the late summer of the year. That's certainly when things wrapped up, although it all began much earlier. She described David Rose as a "robust man of 67." Perhaps to a teenager he seemed robust enough, although he was in fact receiving a disability pension. As early as 1880, the census identified David as being unemployed five months out of the previous twelve, although that may include down time while moving the family from southern to northern

Ohio. But that census also put a checkmark in the column "maimed, crippled and disabled" for David.

One thing Flora remembered that was probably quite accurate was that David Rose's business was trending downward as more and more farmers were able to buy gasoline-powered engines for grinding. The mill was becoming obsolete.

BOY-CRAZY

By the mid-1890s, Celia Rose was a physically mature female. Indeed, she was universally remembered as a big girl for her time: five feet, seven inches tall and 190 pounds in weight. But as her body and natural sexual drive awoke, all she had to control them with was a child's mind. She was able to learn some basic household tasks, including simple cooking and decorative needlework, but it would never truly be enough for her to live independently. Did she know this? Or did the family humor her ambitions to someday grow up to start a family and home of her own?

We don't know. What we do know is that once the adult hormones began flowing, Ceely became fascinated by boys. She would watch boys play ball in the schoolyard, jumping up and down, cheering for anyone who scored. She became fascinated by neighboring farmer Clem Herring, then in his mid-twenties. Following her urges, Ceely wrote a love letter to him and delivered it to him while he was in the field plowing. He thanked her for the note and never said another word about it. In fact, her stealing of the book from the Herrings' mailbox may have been specifically so that she'd have something of his to claim as her own. Herring ignored the gushing letter (which, alas, has apparently not survived), and Ceely's focus began to realign. Next, she delivered another love letter to another handsome farmer, Cary Andrews. He wasn't as kind as Clem Herring and laughed in the girl's face, taunting her. She had to find a different approach to romance.

Ceely's next fixation was on a younger man instead of an older one, but one she still looked up to. Guy Berry was the eldest son of George and Angeline

Guy Berry, *far right*, in an image from around 1890. Also seen are Claude Berry, parents George and Angeline and their younger daughters. In 1896, Guy became Ceely Rose's obsession. *Dr. Robert Berry Collection.*

Berry, the next-door neighbors on the other side of Switzer's Run. They lived in the original house built by Charles Schrack on the hill in front of the mill. By the 1890s, it does not appear to have operated as a general store any more, not least because the Berrys were accumulating what was to become a herd of ten children, filling every corner of the house.

A reporter from the *Chicago Tribune* dug up valley gossip that there had been some sort of falling out between the Roses and Berrys around 1890:

> *The Berrys are prosperous, open-hearted people, with broad acres of well-tilled land, who never quarrel with anyone, and who never feared a quarrel with anyone except the Roses. The peculiar temperament of the pensioner and his family was long ago known to Mr. Berry, and, though Rose's mill is within twenty yards of Berry's front porch, and a conversation can be carried on without difficulty between the two homes, there had been no intercourse between the families in five or six years—no known intercourse. Walter Rose did not speak to George Berry when they passed on the road, and a barely civil salutation sufficed to preserve the form of social amenities when members of the two families met in public.*

Guy Berry was a handsome sixteen-year-old boy, well spoken and attentive to his school lessons. Ceely realized that she could watch his comings and goings at the Berry farm from the windows of the miller's house, both upstairs and down. Attracted to the popular boy, Ceely was soon following him around outside. When she approached him to speak to him, Guy felt sorry for the slow girl who was often teased for her awkwardness. It appears that to be polite, Guy actually responded to Celia and attempted to hold conversations with her.

This was a treatment Ceely never really expected to get from Guy. No handsome man had ever actually responded to her advances. This was a whole new level of engagement for a girl starved for attention from attractive males. Soon she was flat-out smitten. One day, she told him that they would be getting married in three years. Guy expressed surprise and pointed out that he had never agreed to any such thing. Ceely replied that he'd better marry her, or she'd marry one of the three other men who had been trying to kiss her.

"You will be sorry you didn't take me," Ceely said.

"You think so?" the irritated Guy replied. "Just try me."

The following morning, Ceely was waiting for Guy when he came out to feed the horses. She apologized for what she'd said and said he was the only one she had eyes for. Guy shrugged his shoulders.

Guy's little brother Claude, who was annoyed by Ceely's constant fawning after Guy, spoke to Ceely one day when she came looking for her idol.

"Celia," Claude said, "Guy isn't going to marry you. He has got another girl."

This threw her for a moment. Then she pulled herself together. "Then I will marry you, Claude," she said.

"I am too young," he replied. Claude was twelve years old. Ceely said that she was willing to wait until he grew up. Claude thought it ridiculous and told his mother about the conversation.

"She would marry a ten-year-old boy on the spot if she got the chance," Angeline Berry said.

In the late spring of 1896, around mid-May, Guy's patience wore thin, and he stopped being pleasant to Ceely. Although some recountings of the story claim that he lied in order to get Celia to leave him alone, most do not. The accounts that have come down to us paint Guy Berry as a kind boy.

Was it really this simple and pure? Of course, we cannot know the intimate details after all these years. One has to recognize the possibilities for something more untoward happening. How, after all, was Ceely so deadly certain about her attractions? Had she merely developed a certainty of romantic and sexual urges without any education in what was euphemistically called "the facts of life"? Or, like most country children of those days, did she grow up knowing about sex from observing what farm animals did? With the uncomfortable shadows about inbreeding and incest that have run through the rumor mill about this case, one can't deny the possibility that the developmentally disabled young woman had been molested, or even that neighborhood boys had taken advantage of her sheer willingness. One version of the story that appeared in one of the newspaper reports claimed that Guy Berry was a "cheerful idiot" who proposed to Ceely as a joke, and she thought it was for real. That article also bluntly described Celia (misidentified as "Amelia") as "weak-minded" and "easily imposed upon," presumably impressions given to the reporter by valley residents. Like so much in this case, we can't know the exact details of what happened, only probabilities.

All we know for certain is that sometime in early 1896, Ceely crossed a line from fantasizing about a relationship with Guy Berry to believing that they would actually be getting married. Did Guy make her some empty promises in order to take advantage of her? Or was he the unwitting focus of Celia's obsession? We don't know. That Guy was simply trying to be kind to the wayward Ceely remains the most probable unfolding of events. But finally, his patience wore thin.

We do know that Ceely crossed the fantasy line so aggressively that she began to tell other people in the valley that she and Guy were going to be getting married and starting up their own household. She seemed excited with the idea that she would then become the "Maw" of her own place, which suggests that her mother was the true seat of power in the Rose home—and Ceely wanted that kind of power.

Ceely's tales drove Guy to distraction. He appealed to his father for help in shutting up Ceely's story, threatening that if no one could stop the wayward girl, he was going to run away from home to escape it. According to his later testimony, George Berry stomped down the hill to the mill on June 4, 1896, and told David Rose in no uncertain terms to get his daughter under control and keep her away from his boys. He pointed out a window that overlooked Berry's field across Switzer's Run from the mill. Guy was attempting to plow the field with a team of horses, but Ceely was there, begging for the boy's attention.

"Are you going to do something about her pestering my boys?" Berry said.

David's face was red from embarrassment and anger. "I'll stop it," he said, "if I have to lick the whole damned fraternity." He went out onto the deck that jutted out from the back of the mill. "Ceely Rose!" he bellowed. "Get over here right this minute!" George Berry left as Ceely slowly tore herself away from Guy and made her way down to the footbridge that led over the creek. "Stop dawdling," David called. "I want to have a word with you." He turned and walked back into the mill, letting the door slam behind him. Ceely slowly made her way toward the mill.

When Ceely climbed up the stairs and walked into the mill, David unleashed his infamous temper. He came down hard on the girl. He told Celia that she was never to speak to the Berry boys ever again. She was not to follow Guy Berry, not to talk about him, never even to speak his name again in their home. David ranted, but Ceely was used to that. Once he gave her a chance to speak, she begged him not to tell her mother what she had done. Seeing an opportunity, David said that if she behaved and did what he said, he wouldn't say a thing to her mother. Ceely crumpled and promised meekly to behave.

Within a day or two, David had told Rebecca everything, creating a white-hot fury in Celia. When she threatened to do whatever she wanted to do, David responded by saying that as long as he was around, he'd make sure she toed the line.

"You won't be around forever," she sullenly replied. She also displayed resentment against Walter, who joined into the scolding like an additional parent. But immediately afterward, Ceely quietened down and made a noted effort to be more helpful about the house. It must have seemed to the Roses that they had solved the problem and helped their daughter turn a new page and get past the embarrassing sensation she had created. She was finally contributing something positive to their household.

Around this time—we don't know if it was before or after George Berry's visit—Ceely overheard her parents one morning discussing a matter that David had read about in the newspaper. David had been following reports about a murder case from the small Ohio town of Tallmadge, near Akron. In that case, a farmer by the name of Stone, his wife and their hired hand had been bludgeoned to death in March 1896. After a few days of miscellaneous leads, the investigators had settled on a sickly farmhand who used to work for the Stones, named John Smith, as a suspect. Upon interrogation, this "John Smith" confessed under pressure that his real name was Romulus Cotell and that he was a runaway from upstate New York. He had worked for the Stones, but after showing too much interest in their youngest daughter, he was relocated to a neighboring farm. After two days of "sweating" under heavy interrogation, he confessed to the crime, claiming that he meant to

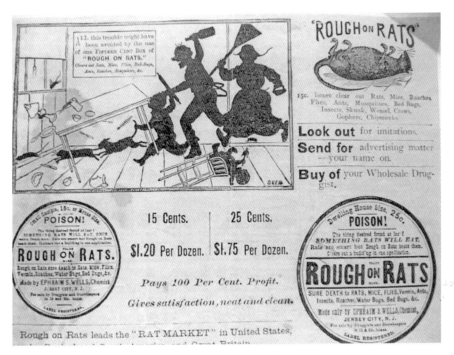

A period newspaper advertisement for Rough-on-Rats brand rat poison, which contained high amounts of arsenic. *Brett J. Mitchell Collection.*

run away with the farmer's daughter after getting the parents out of the way. The farmhand was just another obstacle that had to be removed. It was, in the end, seen as a crime of misguided love, and in April and May 1896, the newspapers were full of the details.

This story stuck with Ceely Rose, and she kept the newspaper to reread the story. She was struck particularly by the idea that lovers could kill someone who was opposed to their union. It made perfect sense to her childish mind. As the brilliant Ohio storyteller Jim Bowsher has said of the case, "Imagine you offer a piece of candy to a child. The child starts to approach to grab the candy, then someone steps in the way. The child will push the person blocking the candy out of the way. For Ceely Rose, Guy Berry was the candy, and she had to remove anyone standing in her path to get to him."

Ceely began brooding on this story. She had the time, after all, as she was no longer allowed to talk endlessly about Guy Berry. One can imagine that she spent a lot of time thinking about Romy Cotell's story during the cool, rainy spring of 1896. Conditions had been so wet that the Roses had begun to have problems with potato bugs around the house and mill, so they sent Walter up to Mansfield in mid-May to buy some Rough-on-Rats rat poison, a popular concoction that used lethal amounts of arsenic mixed with bootblack to give it an unpalatable grayish color, in order to prevent accidental ingestion. Walter bought the poison at Barton's drugstore in downtown Mansfield and then returned home. Rebecca made a solution to spread around the periphery of the house and mill to poison the potato bugs and then distributed it as needed. Afterward, she put the poison into one of her kitchen cabinets for storage. David and Rebecca repeatedly drilled it into Ceely's head that she shouldn't mess with the Rough-on-Rats, as it was a deadly poison. Even a pinch of that stuff could kill a person.

At some point during that rainy spring, Celia Rose put together those two pieces of information: one, that a person could kill people to get them out of the way of love, and two, that Rough-on-Rats would kill a person.

Around June 10, Rebecca intended to put a second dose of poison down for the potato bugs, as the rainy weather had continued. She went to the kitchen cabinet, but no matter how much she searched, she couldn't find the Rough-on-Rats. It was gone.

GRAVE SUSPICIONS

Though unlikely, it is possible that if the Rose family's usual physician, Dr. Budd, had been home on June 24, 1896, we might not be examining this case today. It is fully possible that an older country doctor would have misdiagnosed the family's illness as food poisoning or cholera and seen the whole affair as nothing more than a tragic misfortune. But the first responder on the scene, Dr. John McCombs, came with a different perspective. First trained as a lawyer, Dr. McCombs had subsequently followed that with medical training in Cleveland. By the late nineteenth century, medical schools had shifted to teaching young physicians to be on the lookout for signs of poisoning, which had become a popular—and often subtle—way to murder a target. Older physicians often did not have the training to spot the signs of man-made poisons that had almost the same symptoms as certain illnesses and various natural toxins.

Dr. McCombs, however, was part of this new generation of doctors trained to look for suspicious poisonings. His background in law could only have sharpened these detection skills. McCombs decided very quickly at the Rose house the morning of June 24, 1896, that things weren't adding up. Three family members were violently ill, while the fourth, Celia Rose, was plainly fine.

When Dr. McCombs asked Celia if she had eaten the breakfast along with the rest of the family, she said that she had. He asked her if she was in pain. Ceely said she was. McCombs was unconvinced. When he asked the girl if she had prepared breakfast for the family, the ill Rebecca lifted herself up and interjected that she had prepared the breakfast. When her mother began speaking, Ceely meekly stopped talking.

As the doctor and visiting neighbors who had already heard about the situation nursed the Roses, they found that the three patients were all suffering from terrible thirst, but as soon as they attempted to drink water, violent stomach convulsions forced the water back up. They couldn't keep anything down, including medicines. The severity of their abdominal cramping, plus the inability to take in any water, combined with Ceely Rose's lack of symptoms, convinced Dr. McCombs that something ominous was in the works. As soon as the situation was reasonably in hand, McCombs excused himself, rode back to Newville and stepped into the telegraph office. He wired the office of Richland County sheriff James Boals and Richland County prosecutor Augustus Douglass in Mansfield with his suspicions. Within a short while, they had conferred and sent a response. They said it sounded like food poisoning and to notify them if anything else developed.

Augustus Douglass, originally from Pleasant Valley himself, was the Richland County prosecuting attorney in 1896. *Timothy Brian McKee Collection.*

How could these authorities have displayed such a cavalier attitude to Dr. McCombs's telegram? Perhaps it was a disdain for a country doctor telling them how to do their job. Or perhaps they were suspicious of any lawyer who would quit the practice of the law to go take up the practice of medicine. McCombs himself seemed fully capable of having abrasive run-ins with other officials. In 1900, he was arrested at the order of the Richland County coroner for allegedly procuring an abortion for a woman. After McCombs was acquitted of the charge, he whirled about and sued the coroner for $10,100 in damages. Combative and pugnacious, he later died of a heart attack in 1902, aged only forty-seven.

But the most likely scenario is simply familiarity. Gus Douglass grew up in Pleasant Valley and still owned a farm just up the road from the Roses known as Green Gables, which he returned to on the weekends. It seems likely that in his life as a prominent farmer, lawyer and now county prosecutor, he had likely somewhere crossed paths with the Roses before. His first impression may have been that this humble family was not capable of the sort of life-and-death drama Dr. McCombs was claiming was happening. So, he dismissed the doctor's claim.

Neighbors stopped in and tried to help in any way they could. George and Barbara Davis stopped by and made some herbal tea from the plants in Rebecca's herb garden. Perhaps Rebecca was able to at least sip on a little of the tea, as her poisoning did not appear to be as severe as that of David and Walter, for she could sit up, whereas David was laid out on the sofa in the front parlor and Walter was resting on a cot in the tiny house's back parlor.

The evening of the day the Roses became sick, neighbor George Berry was leaving the house. Living next door, he cut through the yard instead of walking up to the road. As he did so, he suddenly noticed vague shapes in the grass around his feet. There were several of the Roses' chickens, lying dead in the yard.

The following day, family physician Dr. Allen Budd returned to town and took over the case. Dr. Budd had attended the Roses a number of times over the years since the family moved to Pleasant Valley, mostly dealing with David's various ailments related to his Civil War service, although he had also treated Celia for malaria at one point. But his affidavit in support of David Rose's disability pension application stated that Budd had only attended the family half a dozen times over the decade and a half that they had lived in Pleasant Valley.

Not wanting to merely take Dr. McCombs's word, Dr. Budd made his own assessment of the situation, ruling out the possibility of a bilious attack in David's case, considering his medical history. Dr. Budd asked the family about the possibility of poison, which none of them wanted to admit was a possibility. As the patients continued to struggle, though, Dr. Budd called in Drs. John Culler and Samuel Alban to join him and Dr. McCombs for a consult. Coming to the conclusion that the Roses had, in fact, been poisoned, Budd, McCombs, Culler and Alban began administering iron as an antidote to probable arsenical poisoning, but this was not until five days after the poisoning with no improvement in David or Walter.

David Rose slipped in and out of consciousness, tossing and turning in pain as he muttered and groaned. For six days, he had struggled. The iron treatments were too little, too late. Late on the night of Tuesday, June 30, he died. Early the following morning, word was sent for the undertaker/coffinmaker who lived in Lucas, Jacob Marks, to come prepare the body for burial. But first, Drs. Budd, Culler and McCombs were joined by Richland County coroner George W. Baughman. An autopsy was to be done.

Richland County coroner
George W. Baughman.
*John Sherman Room at the
Mansfield/Richland County
Public Library.*

David's stiff body was laid out on boards in the front parlor. Due to the lack of space and the inability of the other victims to retire to the upstairs bedrooms, they may indeed have overheard the progress of the autopsy from the adjoining rooms, although Rebecca wasn't officially notified of David's death for fear of the shock killing her.

Coroner Baughman noticed that there were burn-like eruptions around David's mouth, where he had vomited repeatedly. The doctors noted that this would be expected with a heavy metal poisoning, such as arsenic. David's stomach and intestines were removed, examined and preserved in jars. Visual inspection showed the stomach to be badly inflamed and rigid, both strong signs of arsenical poisoning.

Even though this was an age before modern forensics, there was one test available to investigators to prove arsenical poisoning—the Marsh test—but it was expensive. One of the doctors wired county officials in Mansfield to ask permission to send the old man's stomach for a Marsh test. The county commissioners, not yet convinced it was murder, declined. The coroner took the preserved organ with him and returned to town. The other doctors returned to treating the survivors. The procession for David's funeral left the miller's house and marched a mile up the road, where the service was held at Pleasant Valley Lutheran Church, with Pastor O.E. Kramer officiating. Immediately afterward, David S. Rose was buried at the church graveyard in a plot prepared by his neighbors.

For almost another week, the horrible limbo at the Rose house continued, with Rebecca making miniscule progress toward healing and Walter slipping further and further away. Angeline Schrack Heier recalled years later that she normally went barefoot around the valley in the summertime and found that the little tan slippers she was made to wear for the funeral had worn a blister on her heel. When her mother told her after the service to run a container of Balm of Gilead salve for Walter's sore lips down to the Rose home, Angeline protested about her blister. Her mother told her to take off the slippers and go.

As Angeline hesitantly entered the miller's house, she saw Walter on a cot in the back parlor. Even after many decades, the image still haunted her: "I

David Rose's pension file from the National Archives after his murder. There is no sentimentality in government paperwork. *Author's collection.*

can still see how terrible Walter's lips looked. But the mother had sufficiently recovered to be dressed in a black dress, lying on a bed in the bedroom and fanning with a black fan. It was midsummer and very hot. I felt good about my errand when she called me to her bedside, put her arm around me and told me what a good little girl I was to bring the salve to Walter." It isn't clear exactly where this bed was that Angeline refers to, as Rebecca was likely still too weak to climb up to the second floor. If Walter was on a cot in the parlor, it is possible that Rebecca was now resting on the sofa on which her husband had passed in the front parlor. Alternately, it is possible that helpful neighbors might even have brought her bed downstairs for her recuperation.

Walter continued to decline. Unable to keep water down, he was progressively dying of dehydration, even though doctors and neighbors kept wetting his dried, cracking lips in an attempt to get some water into his system. But he was too far gone. Walter W. Rose died on Independence Day.

By this point, residents in the valley were in an uproar that the body count was mounting while the officials in Mansfield were still doing nothing. A flurry of telegrams and an article in the *Mansfield Daily*

Shield titled "Grave Suspicions" goaded the authorities into action. The attending doctors autopsied Walter with the same findings and asked again for permission to have his organs given the Marsh test. The county commissioners gave permission for the preserved stomach of David Rose to be tested but noted that Walter's entrails could be tested only in the event that David's test proved positive.

There was a very real chance that the Marsh test, performed by chemists Drs. Erwin and Speer in Mansfield, would yield an indeterminate result, considering that David did not die until six days after the alleged poisoning, and then his entrails had rested another five days before testing began. Arsenic does not always maintain well in tissues, although if it is there in spectacular amounts, it can actually have a preserving effect on the tissue. The testing would take a week.

Meanwhile, the situation had already grown too explosive for the authorities to ignore it any longer. The investigation was underway.

THE INVESTIGATION BEGINS

Richland County prosecutor Augustus Douglass belatedly realized that he had a bad public relations situation on his hands. The newspapers had been following the Rose case and seizing on every rumor that it was going to turn out to be a murder case. Coroner Baughman had already made a spectacular gaffe to the media. When asked if he thought it was true that Celia Rose was mentally slow, Baughman opined that the girl was "not altogether *compos mentis*" and that the rest of the family were "all very dull in perception." Whatever the coroner's personal opinions, this public expression of them could hurt any attempt to get a conviction in a court of law on a charge of murder in the first degree.

Sheriff James Boals appears to have elected to let Douglass spearhead the investigation. As the sheriff of one of the larger counties in Ohio, and one that straddles the borderlands between the northwestern farmlands and the southeastern hills, Boals had his work cut out for him. He defaulted to the role of law enforcement officer carrying out the prosecutor's instructions.

Augustus Douglass was later remembered by writer Louis Bromfield in his book *Pleasant Valley* as "a brilliant but eccentric lawyer whose own sense of mockery and humor destroyed his respect for legal processes and blighted what might have been a great but a far less human and satisfactory career." Bromfield remembered those qualities in connection to his cousin Phoebe Wise, a legendary Mansfield eccentric who was good friends with Gus Douglass. Where many people in Mansfield found Phoebe Wise scandalous and beyond the pale—between her wearing old ball gowns and dragging the trail behind her in the dirt, dressing up in men's overalls to do yardwork or profanely cussing out people who gave her funny looks— Douglass recognized that the peculiar woman was mentally sharp and profound, something of a kindred spirit.

As Gus Douglass was known for his wit and sense of humor, it was also sometimes played back on him. On one occasion shortly after the Ceely Rose case, two Mansfield lawyers— Allen Beach and Gus's opposing counsel from the Ceely trial, Jim Reed—decided to take the afternoon off and go hunting. While they weren't particularly adamant about hunting, they figured it would be best to put in a good show by taking rifles out for the hunt and using

Richland County sheriff James F. Boals. *Timothy Brian McKee Collection.*

that as an excuse to drop in somewhere and invite themselves to dinner at one of their friends' houses out in the countryside southeast of town.

The problem for Beach and Reed was that neither of them had a gun handy. Reed asked around and found an ancient flintlock he could borrow, but Beach was initially unsuccessful. It occurred to Reed that Gus Douglass would probably have something at his house in town, so they proceeded there, even though they assumed Gus was at work in his office in the county courthouse. Since Beach was the one without a weapon, Reed refused to go begging and sent Beach to the door.

Mrs. Douglass answered the attorney's knock.

"I've come for Gus's gun," Beach said, describing the outing he and Reed were taking that afternoon.

"All right," she said. "I suppose you got permission from Mr. Douglass to get it."

"Oh, I've talked to Gus about that gun," the attorney deftly said. She invited him in and fetched the gun. Beach and Reed proceeded to head south out of town, when who should they see driving in their direction but Gus Douglass himself. Beach flipped the end of his long coat over the rifle before hailing the prosecutor. After a few pleasantries, Beach asked Douglass if he could borrow Gus's rifle for their hunting expedition.

"Well, I don't generally loan that gun, but if you'll agree to bring it back in just the condition you get it, you may have it," Gus said. The two buggies continued on their way, the lawyers heading out toward Pleasant Valley, southeast of town, and Douglass proceeding directly to his house. There his wife informed him that a red-bearded lawyer had been by to borrow his gun and was that all right?

"How in thunder did those fellows get here so quick?" he said. "They were going in the opposite direction the last I saw of them." A tell-all item appeared the following day in the local paper revealing the joke.

But sense of humor or not, Douglass's reluctance to take the Pleasant Valley situation seriously had let it blow up into a scandal, and it would prove to be the rock on which his career as a politician foundered. In fact, Douglass's reluctance likely stemmed from his quick realization that if it was, in fact, a true poisoning case, it would be very difficult to win a prosecution against Ceely Rose. By its very nature as a relatively slow-acting form of murder, poisoning requires planning. That means it must be prosecuted as premeditated murder in the first degree. Particularly if Gus Douglass already knew who Ceely Rose was, he would have instantly seen that it would be difficult to prove her sane and capable of sophisticated planning in a court of law. But ignoring the case had not caused it to go away. He had to do something. After Walter's autopsy and funeral were out of the way, Douglass trundled down Pleasant Valley to begin questioning people on July 7.

Douglass asked Sheriff Boals and his deputies to search every inch of the house and the mill to find the poison. The initial suspicion was that Ceely had soaked arsenic flypaper in water and then used the water to make the coffee she served the family on June 24. But a search of the buildings turned up nothing. As public speculation had already run so far in the direction of intentional poisoning, the coroner, Dr. Baughman, made a statement to the press on July 6, cautioning them that the symptoms of arsenic poisoning and acute, fatal gastritis were indistinguishable without the final results of the Marsh test. Then he again demonstrated his lack of savvy with the media by going ahead and stating that he believed it was intentional poisoning.

Douglass decided to hold a formal inquest in the Valley Hall School. Although newspaper reports make no mention of it, Bromfield claimed in his retelling of the case that Guy Berry had been sent out of the area until events settled down, which might be true considering that he never testified at Ceely's later trial. It was certainly some favoritism, though, if the authorities let him avoid answering questions and testifying. The newspapers merely stated that Celia, her mother and eight others testified at the inquest. Two valley residents, unidentified in the press, got so animated in their argument about whether or not Ceely Rose was guilty that it almost escalated into a fistfight. Later testimony at Celia's trial would suggest that one of the combatants was probably valley resident Wesley McDermott, who suggested lynching the girl. Prosecutor Douglass calmed tempers down and asked the people of the valley to let the investigation run its course to uncover the truth.

The star witness everyone wanted to hear from was, naturally, Ceely Rose herself. But Douglass started his questions with other people, including one neighbor who had heard that Celia had either prepared the breakfast or helped her mother prepare it by fetching the cottage cheese—what was known in the valley in those days as smear case (from the German phrase *schmeer käse*)—from the springhouse. When Rebecca Rose testified, she said that she had prepared the entire breakfast and specifically denied that Celia had helped her with any part of it. No matter how many ways Prosecutor Douglass asked her that question, the woman, though physically weak, displayed an iron will.

So, finally, the prosecutor moved on to Ceely herself. While the young woman liked being the center of attention, the presence of so many people peering intensely at her brought out her latent stuttering when Douglass began asking her questions, particularly when he raised his voice.

When Douglass asked Ceely about the breakfast food preparation, she turned and looked at her mother, who nodded her head. Ceely proceeded to give a carefully worded answer that sounded well practiced. When she finished, she looked again at her mother, who nodded approval. In between other questions, Douglass kept circling back around and asking the food preparation question in different ways. Each time, Ceely gave the rehearsed answer, with coaching from her mother. Rebecca Rose had clearly decided that even if her daughter was guilty, she had to be protected.

Douglass almost caught the young woman when he offhandedly said, "But Ceely, *why* did you put that stuff in the coffee that morning for breakfast?"

"Because I wanted to," she stammered, then caught herself and said, "but I didn't put it there, though." Even her correction was not a clear refutation of the crime, for it was to emerge later that it wasn't the coffee at all that was poisoned. It was the cottage cheese.

Without a confession from the girl, and with the mother actively hindering the investigation, the authorities were stymied, unable to assemble a winnable case against Ceely Rose. While they had motive and opportunity, the young woman's mental acuity was in question, and they had yet to gather any physical evidence.

That came with the return of the Marsh test from Cleveland. As soon as Douglass, Sheriff Boals and Coroner Baughman examined the test report, an order was immediately sent back to Drs. Erwin and Speer to perform the same test on Walter's organs. The first Marsh test had indicated that David died not merely from arsenical poisoning, but rather from "massive arsenical poisoning." There was enough arsenic in his stomach to have killed several people.

Gus Douglass now officially had a murder case on his hands.

THE INVESTIGATION STALLS

Unfortunately, the first physical evidence in the case proved nothing more than what most people had already suspected. Mind you, there were still heated arguments among valley residents. The Ohler family was convinced that giggly Ceely Rose was incapable of such monstrous designs and defended her vigorously. Wesley McDermott was convinced that the odd girl was guilty because she had always seemed "off" to him. Flora Schrack later wrote that although she was skeptical of Ceely's innocence, she also had difficulty wrapping her head around the idea that Ceely Rose would be capable of planning and executing murder. She didn't seem sophisticated enough. Her sister Angeline wrote in her recollection, "Subnormals are sometimes very shrewd[.]"

It took a week for Walter's Marsh test to come back. It confirmed what was expected—that he, too, had died of massive arsenical poisoning. Douglass's murder investigation immediately turned into a double homicide case. But additional questioning did nothing to budge Ceely and her mother from their stubborn insistence that Rebecca had prepared the breakfast and Ceely knew nothing about it. Rebecca had no conceivable motive to be the murderer herself, and her coaching of Ceely made it clear that she was attempting to shield the slow girl. Without a confession of some sort, the prosecutor had no proof that it was Ceely who did the poisoning. A defense counsel would no doubt argue that anyone with a grudge could have snuck into the Roses' springhouse and poisoned their food. The circumstantial case was weak, and a weak case would not prove premeditated murder.

Not knowing what else to do, Gus Douglass made a controversial decision. He and the sheriff's deputies backed off and left Ceely alone with her mother in the miller's house. While neighbors still checked in regularly, this left the young woman and her mother alone much of the time. To the surprise of those who suspected the girl of having poisoned her family, she relished the role of caretaker. Ceely became more active and useful than she had ever been before, preparing her own food and patiently feeding Rebecca buttermilk until the old woman was able to begin downing soft food the week after Walter died. Friends and neighbors helped, but much of the food preparation was done by Ceely.

WITH GROWING CONFIDENCE IN the kitchen and time on her own, Ceely undertook some new projects. Late one mid-July morning, George and Angeline Berry heard a knock on their front door. Opening the door, George found Ceely Rose standing there, holding something covered with a towel. After greeting the parents of her beloved, she got right to the point.

"I baked this pie for you and Mrs. Berry," Celia said, holding it out. "But it's only for you two. Guy's not allowed to eat any of this pie, all right?"

Berry uncertainly took the pie and thanked the strange girl. She merrily returned to the miller's house. George explained to his wife what the Rose girl had said. They agreed immediately that there was no way in the world that they were going to touch that pie. So, George walked to the back side of the house, out of sight of the Rose cottage, and flung the suspicious pie out into the yard without a further thought.

Later that day, Angeline Berry stepped out the back door to shake out a rug. She noticed on the ground the remains of Ceely's pie, with dozens of small, triangular peck marks in it. She looked up and saw all their chickens, lying dead throughout the yard. If this story was told to the investigators at the time, it never made its way into the newspaper. The story has been carried through generations of the Berry family down to this day.

Back at home, Ceely wasn't done with her kitchen projects. One of the regular visitors since trouble began was Pastor Kramer from the Pleasant Valley Lutheran Church, who came by once a week to check on things and pray with Rebecca. This week, Ceely fried up a specially seasoned chicken for the pastor, but alas, he had another sick parishioner to visit and ended up skipping a week.

On days when Rebecca felt like sitting up, she'd talk with visitors. While she had never officially been informed of the deaths of David and Walter, one of the neighbors had explained to her what had happened before she was taken down the road to the inquest. On these days with visitors, she would often speak tearfully of "Pappy's last day of grinding" at the mill. As the month wore on, being taken care of by Ceely, Rebecca began to slowly regain her strength, although she could still ingest only soft food.

One day during the third week of the month, Dr. Budd informed Rebecca that it was finally clear that she was going to survive. He cautioned her that her recovery would be gradual and slow, but in time, she would get back to something approaching normal. Rebecca was pleased and relieved.

Celia overheard the doctor.

We don't know what conversation may have passed between Rebecca and her daughter between the doctor's visit and his emergency return the following evening. If Rebecca thought that Celia had given up her fantasies about Guy Berry and was prepared to go on living a life like it had always been, with Rebecca now the sole authority figure in charge of the girl, she was mistaken. Ceely was just as convinced as ever that Guy would someday take her away and marry her.

Did Rebecca perhaps suggest that they would move away from the sad memories of Pleasant Valley and go elsewhere, either to ancestral roots down in southern Ohio or perhaps to a fresh start some place where no one knew them? It's certainly possible. If she did, that would have struck Celia as an emergency, something that she had to immediately stop—after all, how could Guy come and take her away if she wasn't there for him to rescue? She would wait a lifetime for Guy if she had to, but it had to be right there, where he could find her.

Or it may have simply been a desire to finish the plan she had started weeks ago. While Celia clearly had more affection for her mother than she had ever shown for her father or brother, she still saw her as an obstacle standing between her and Guy Berry. All obstacles had to go.

The afternoon of July 18, 1896, Rebecca asked her daughter for some bread and milk (perhaps the more Appalachian cornbread and buttermilk, misreported by northern reporters?). Ceely got the milk from the springhouse in the yard under the giant elm tree and brought it in to her mother. Rebecca relished the food and ate heartily for the first time in almost a month. Her appetite had returned so much that she asked her daughter to fetch her seconds. Celia did so.

A few bites into the milk-soaked bread of the second serving, Rebecca frowned and said to Ceely that the flavor of the milk seemed a bit off from how it tasted in the first serving. She paused, then resumed eating. She didn't eat much more before she quit. Within a few hours, she had returned to full poisoning symptoms and started vomiting again. Ceely later said it was all she could do not to laugh at the sight of it, suggesting that in addition to her learning disability, she may have had some degree of borderline personality disorder. A neighbor dropping in discovered the situation and sent for help. Grandma Schrack, Clem Herring and his mother, Phebe, came at a run to the miller's house.

At one point, Rebecca peered up from her bed at her wayward daughter. "Ceely, if it's you that's done this, God help you," she said. The girl protested that she hadn't done anything. Rebecca gave her a stern look. "Look me in the face, child, and tell me the truth," the old woman said.

Ceely hung her head and silently walked out of the room.

DR. BUDD WAS SENT for from Perrysville, and he arrived shortly. Unfortunately, there was little he could do for the already weakened woman, who grew progressively worse as the night wore on. He sent someone to send an urgent telegram to Prosecutor Douglass and Sheriff Boals while he tried to ease Rebecca's pain.

Clem Herring and his mother grabbed pencil and paper and wrote out Rebecca's thoughts for her last will and testament, for she realized sharply that she was unlikely to see the dawn. Amazingly, even in light of almost certainly knowing that Ceely had poisoned her not once but twice, she put Ceely in her will. Rebecca directed that the family's assets be auctioned off, and after all bills were paid, any remaining sum should be split evenly between Ceely and Rebecca's grandson, John Long.

In the darkest hours of the night, Rebecca Rose breathed her last, with her neighbors and her killer waiting at her bedside.

TO CATCH A KILLER

The usual postmortem activities of autopsy and testing were immediately undertaken. The authorities once again descended on the valley with questions and procured equally fruitless results as in previous efforts. To the prosecutor's extreme embarrassment, it appeared they were being outwitted by a simpleton.

Ceely seemed indifferent to the idea of staying alone in the miller's house, but Prosecutor Douglass quickly became aware of the furor arising in the valley. Residents were beginning to ask how many people would have to die before the sheriff and prosecutor would actually do something about Ceely Rose?

Douglass had identified in his earlier interviews that the Ohler family, who lived near his farm, Green Gables, on Pleasant Valley Road, were Ceely's most outspoken supporters. Jane Ohler in particular refused to believe that a giggly girl like Ceely Rose was capable of premeditated murder. Douglass asked the Ohlers if they would take Ceely in. If there was any hesitation in their agreement to do so, it wasn't recorded in any of the surviving sources. Ceely was immediately moved up to the Ohler farm, just beyond Pipe's Cliff and the Pleasant Valley Lutheran Church, where she promptly fell into a lifestyle of lying on the sofa reading while others around her took care of household chores.

At this point, Douglass began a slow-burn strategy of penetrating Ceely's dull defenses with something that would appeal to her selfish emotions: a friend. While he was inspecting the miller's house once again for the poison

John and Jane Ohler, Ceely's defenders, took her in after her family was dead. *John Sherman Room at the Mansfield/Richland County Public Library.*

that Ceely seemed to make magically disappear after each murder, Douglass had been approached by George Davis, who lived farther up Hastings Road. Davis pointed out that his daughter Tracy, a few years younger than Ceely, had gone to Valley Hall School with the girl and had taken her under her wing a number of times in the past because she felt sorry for the slow girl, who often got picked on by less sensitive children. Davis offered his daughter's services as a friend who might be able to get Celia to talk.

Douglass pursued his usual activities first and made the rounds questioning people, including Ceely, who was as stubbornly unhelpful as ever. When neither questions nor searches turned up any new evidence, Douglass stepped back and pondered the situation. Without a confession from Ceely Rose, a premeditated murder charge against her was almost certainly doomed to fail. Many people were convinced that she wasn't mentally together enough to be responsible for her own actions.

A lot of people in the valley were saying they thought Ceely was insane and that they'd support her being sent off to the state hospital in Toledo if it ended her reign of terror in the valley. But Douglass didn't have that option. Poisoning takes planning. Planning means she had to be charged with murder in the first degree. His only chance of making a jury agree that Celia Rose was sane enough to know what she was doing would be to get a confession. If Douglass didn't make that happen, he might lose control of the situation entirely. He must have feared that mob violence might rear up, with the farmers of the valley taking the law into their own hands and lynching the girl. Augustus Douglass finally sent word to George Davis to come meet him at Green Gables to discuss the idea of slowly easing a confession out of the murderer.

George Davis and his family had known the Roses since they moved into Pleasant Valley. Their children attended school together, the families attended church together and there was traffic back and forth between their houses. George and his wife, Barbara, had tried to be good neighbors and help out the Roses when the illnesses struck. But like many, they were uncomfortable with Celia's lack of illness and, even more so, her apparent lack of concern with events. They had known her for years, and many times she had visited the Davis farm on Hastings Road at the invitation of their daughter Tracy, three years younger than Ceely but one whom Ceely looked up to.

Ceely knew the other Davis children as well, including Cora, Tracy's younger sister. While the Davises were visiting the Roses to help care for them during the illnesses, Cora at one point said something to Ceely that caused Ceely to say something suspicious. Frustratingly, transcripts of the trial have not survived, and newspaper coverage says just this, without detailing what the comment was. Whatever it was, it was enough to prompt George Davis to believe that the Rose girl was guilty. He told the sheriff and prosecutor about what he had heard, but it wasn't sufficient evidence to provoke an arrest leading to prosecution. More was needed.

By 1896, George's daughter Tracy, nineteen, was working as a clerk in a store in Bellville, Ohio, about fifteen miles away. Tracy heard all about the lurid story of the poisonings from the newspapers, but she hadn't had a chance to visit the Roses. She did visit home one weekend, and her father said that he was concerned that without some sort of confession from Celia, the case might never be solved. Davis asked his daughter if she would be willing to try to get the confession from Ceely. Tracy said she'd do it. That was when Davis first approached Prosecutor Douglass about helping, after the second death. Douglass did not take up Davis's offer until Rebecca died as well.

At Green Gables, George Davis asked if there was a reward to compensate his daughter for the work she'd lose in undertaking this effort. Douglass replied that he could offer no reward. Davis nonetheless later testified that he thought his daughter would at least be paid for her time, which she apparently was not. But Davis called on his daughter to come home from Bellville and help.

Tracy Davis. Slightly younger than Ceely Rose, Davis had nonetheless recognized her schoolmate's basic childishness and had taken her under her wing. Tracy would be the one to finally draw out Ceely's confession. *James Reed Collection.*

The plan that George Davis and Gus Douglass had devised was for Tracy to meet with Ceely and simply talk. After renewing their friendship, Tracy was to only slowly advance any questions about the case if Ceely was comfortable and forthcoming with her. When it seemed like an opportunity was beginning to open, Tracy should stay with Ceely for a few days at the Ohler home and continue to work on her. When it seemed like Ceely was nearing the level of openness where she might confess, Tracy was to tell Ceely a story: she was to confess that she was in love with a young man but that her parents wouldn't let her see him. Then she was to ask Ceely for advice on what she should do.

The plan was started slowly by having Tracy visit Ceely at the Ohlers' the day after Rebecca Rose was buried. Ceely was delighted to see her old friend, whom she hadn't seen in some time, and they walked out in the Ohler farmyard as they chatted.

Tracy pressed for information too fast. She asked Ceely if she had anything to do with that funny business about poison. Ceely turned her head slowly and gave Tracy a long, hard stare.

"I know how it was done," Ceely said, then paused, still staring. "If you don't tell anyone, maybe I'll tell you in a week." That was all Ceely had to say at the time.

Tracy visited again, staying a few days, around July 25. The girls talked extensively and took walks around the valley. Ceely mentioned that once, she went down to visit Guy Berry. Tracy asked her if she had anything else she wanted to talk about and reassured her that talking about other things might make her feel better. Ceely ventured nothing else.

It isn't known if Ceely's claim about visiting Guy Berry is true or fantasy. Jane Ohler did testify that at one point during Tracy's visit Ceely said she was homesick and expressed a desire to go back down to her house. Mrs. Ohler asked her why she wanted to do that.

Ceely replied that she missed the old mill and the chickens. While we know that Ceely poisoned some of their chickens, the later estate sale records indicate that the Roses had sixty remaining chickens. They were soon to be auctioned off at the sale, which was to take place on August 15. Ceely was apparently unaware of the pending sale.

But the chickens probably didn't figure much in Ceely's desire to visit the mill. What was also near there was Guy Berry. While things remained in limbo with Ceely, George Berry had instructed his son to feed the Roses' five hogs. Thus, it may well be that Celia's entire motivation for visiting the miller's house was to chance upon seeing Guy Berry. Whether she did or not was not recorded.

Mrs. Ohler asked Tracy to walk with the girl down to the mill on one of their walks. Tracy led Celia down Pleasant Valley Road but noticed something when she and the girl walked past the Pleasant Valley Lutheran Church graveyard, on the way to the mill. Ceely's family were buried in a plot of fresh graves right next to the road. As they passed, Ceely glanced indifferently at the turned-up earth and made no comment. That startled and chilled Tracy. She grew more determined to get the story.

On the way back, Tracy suggested taking a break for a moment. The girls sat down on a big, smooth, waterworn limestone rock on the roadside near Valley Hall School, where they had been classmates. Tracy asked Ceely if she had anything she wanted to talk about. Ceely said she'd think it over and let her know. Tracy returned home that evening and gave her father a progress report.

On July 30, Tracy tried it again, this time showing up unannounced, to throw Ceely a little off balance. She showed up late in the afternoon, announcing that she'd like to stay all night. This apparently didn't faze Mrs. Ohler, who welcomed her. Perhaps Tracy offered to help out with chores, something Ceely never did. The girls stayed up late talking. Ceely asked Tracy for any news about Guy or any of the other boys at school. Tracy had none.

The tombstone purchased for the Rose family plot by estate executor Clem Herring after Rebecca Rose's death. *Author's collection.*

After breakfast the following morning, Tracy asked Ceely where she wanted to walk, and Ceely said she'd like to go down to the churchyard. The young women walked down Pleasant Valley Road, passing Pipe's Cliff, and then walked past the church and over to the graveyard, just before the gasworks.

The girls stood next to the unmarked graves. Grass was already starting to grow over David Rose's grave and was just creeping in on Walter's. Rebecca's grave was still freshly packed. A stone would only be bought for the graves after Clem Herring wrapped up the rest of the estate business and the probate court judge authorized him to purchase a tombstone "not exceeding one hundred dollars in cost." That is the large stone that remains there today.

Celia dropped to her knees, folded her hands and began praying. Tracy must have been startled for a moment, perhaps thinking that Ceely was overcome. But she wasn't. Kneeling was how she had been taught by her mother, and that's how she would continue to pray the rest of her life.

After they stood, the girls went over to the church and sat down on the front steps, looking out over the rich fields of the valley, ripening toward harvest.

"Do you miss them?" Tracy said. Ceely paused for a moment, thinking.

"I miss Maw," she said.

Nothing more forthcoming, Tracy decided to circle back around. She reminded Ceely of her promise from the first time Tracy visited her. Ceely gave her another long, hard look. Then she relaxed a little.

"I guess you didn't tell anyone what I said," Celia said. "You didn't tell anyone I went and saw Guy, either." She paused for a long time, thinking. But still she didn't talk.

Tracy knew that this was the moment she would either get the confession or fail. "Ceely, can I tell you a secret of mine? I need to ask for your advice about it," she said. Ceely was surprised, intrigued and flattered to be asked for advice.

"Sure," she said. Tracy proceeded to tell the fake story about unrequited love that the prosecutor and her father had devised for her to use to trick Ceely. She said that she was in love with a handsome young man, but her parents were against it and were forbidding her to see him, even speak his name. Ceely listened in wide-eyed wonder.

"I just don't know what to do," Tracy finished. "What would you do if you were in my situation?"

Ceely paused a long moment. "I'd kill them," she suddenly said. "That's what I did." This was it. She was finally coming clean with the story. Tracy knew she had to keep it coming.

"How did you do it?"

"I put Rough-on-Rats in the smear case," she said, pleased with herself.

"Not the coffee or the cherries?"

"No, I confounded them lawmen."

"Where did you get it?" Tracy asked.

Ceely paused, staring forward. "It was Guy," Ceely said quickly, without looking at her friend. "He got that stuff. It was all his idea."

"Really?" Tracy said, startled.

"Um. Yes," Ceely said.

Tracy gathered her thoughts and continued on. "Where did you hide the poison? The sheriff never did find it."

Ceely laughed. "I was too smart for them," she said. "I put it in a pepper box and hid it under a dock leaf in the yard. I guess it's still there. Want to go see?"

The steps of the Pleasant Valley Lutheran Church, where Ceely first confessed her crime to Tracy Davis. *Author's collection.*

Tracy did, so they walked down the road to the miller's house. Ceely ran into the yard to the side of the springhouse that faced away from the house. There, she reached under a huge burdock leaf—a plant also known locally as pigweed—and pulled out a metal tin. She opened it up and showed it to Tracy.

"It's empty," Tracy said.

"Yes, I used the last of it on Maw," Ceely said. She looked more closely at the box. "I thought I got all that stuff out, but there's a little bit left." She held the tin out to Tracy, who saw that traces of the rat poison had stuck in the corners of the metal container.

"Do you want it?" Ceely said.

Tracy almost said no, but then she realized the prosecutor might need it. "Yes, I'll—I'll save it as a keepsake," Tracy said.

"Oh, good," Ceely said, pleased.

"Maybe I'd better get you back up to Mrs. Ohler's," Tracy said.

"You could stay all night again if you want to," Ceely said. Tracy made up an excuse, saying she had to get back home. She walked Ceely back up Pleasant Valley Road. At home, Tracy told her father what Ceely said and showed him the tin.

"Let's go see if Gus Douglass is home," George Davis said.

The county prosecutor wasn't at home, but Davis was able to reach him in the city by telegram and arrange a meeting. They discussed what Tracy had found, and he showed Douglass the pepper box. The prosecutor was impressed that Tracy had gotten Celia to turn over the box to her. Douglass took possession of it so that he could send it to the chemists, so see if they could test the powdery traces that remained inside the box. But he stressed that the box in itself still wasn't adequate proof, especially if it was empty. Douglass explained that to take the case to prosecution, they would need another witness to Ceely Rose's confession, someone willing to hide in a prearranged position, let Tracy draw Ceely there and get her to talk again so that the witness could listen to the story and be willing to testify for the trial. Without that second witness, the story was just hearsay. The prosecutor looked right at Mr. Davis. Davis said he'd do it.

The surviving sources do not agree on exactly what day the case turned. It was somewhere around August 1, 1896, although the news wasn't broken out in the newspapers until a week and a half later. But the gist of it was that the prosecutor and George Davis instructed Tracy to visit Ceely again at the Ohler farm and take her for another walk, this time ending up inside the Ohler's barn.

Tracy's father, meanwhile, had snuck onto the Ohler barn and secreted himself in the haymow in the upper part of the barn. Tracy was to bring Ceely in and get her in a spot where the girls' conversation could be heard from the hayloft. Some sources claim that Davis also had pencil and paper with him, to take notes about what Ceely was saying, although it isn't clear if this was actually the case or if he wrote down his recollections later. After all, the scribbling of a pencil is a sound that might carry through a quiet barn.

Opening the barn door, Tracy saw that the Ohlers' buggy was in its usual place, just under the front opening of the haymow. She suggested to Ceely that they sit in the buggy and talk. As they walked toward the buggy, Tracy couldn't help but peer up into the dim loft. She could see some bales of hay stacked toward the front of the mow, but she couldn't see if her father was there or not. She hoped he was.

The girls sat down. Tracy brought up the subject of their previous discussion.

"You haven't told no one," Ceely said.

"Well, you told me not to tell," Tracy said carefully.

"Yes. But I got to tell you, I feel awfully bad about one thing I said. I ain't slept well since I talked to you."

Tracy turned and peered at Ceely in the silent gloom of the barn. It was a rare moment when Ceely actually looked troubled. George Berry leaned forward from his hiding spot ten feet above the girls and peered down at them. Ceely showed no sign whatsoever of worrying if anyone else was around, remaining face-forward the whole time she talked, as if driving the buggy herself.

"I lied about Guy Berry," Celia said. "He didn't have nothing to do with any of it. I been thinking about it, and I would feel awful if he got into trouble on my account. I did it all myself."

Tracy sighed a little in relief. "Then where did you get the rat poison?"

"Oh, we had that. Maw sent Walter up to the drug store in Mansfield for that. She put it out for tater bugs, but she had some left. She put it in the kitchen cabinet, so I took and put it in that pepper box to keep it dry. See, I couldn't keep it inside the springhouse, cause everybody is always in and out. I put it in the pepper tin under a dock leaf outside and nobody ever seen it."

Ceely laughed. "I got scared when Maw went looking for it one day. She yelled at Paw up-and-down, said he must have took it out to the mill. Paw said he took the box out, spread a little, and put it back. They fought like cats and dogs about that. They never did figure out I took it."

"Ceely, if Guy didn't tell you to do this, who did?"

Ceely stopped laughing and looked straight ahead for so long, Tracy thought she had somehow not heard her. But suddenly she started speaking, not quietly like a confession but perfectly plain and straightforward in manner.

"The devil," Ceely said. "Maw told all about the Bible and the Devil. She said that Devil would come to you and put bad thoughts in your head, and you had to push him down and not let him do that. After they scolded me so, I guess I didn't want to push him down no more.

"I said all that about Guy cause I don't want to give myself away like that Romy Cotell did. He talked and said it all. I knew if I told you the devil told me to do it, I'd give myself away."

"So, Guy knew nothing about this?" Tracy said.

Ceely paused. "No," she said. "I told him my folks would be going away soon. I told him that black wagon would come and take them away."

"Black wagon?"

"That black wagon. I told him it would come from Lucas to get them and go right by his house." A chill must have run down Tracy's back as she realized Ceely was talking about the funeral hearse.

"Did he ask you to explain that more?" Tracy said.

"No, he just told me not to say things like that. I asked him if he got the medicine."

Tracy turned and looked at Celia. "Medicine? What medicine."

"He was supposed to get something that would keep me from being *enciente*."

Tracy's face burned. She was surprised Ceely knew that word. It was the polite French word for "expecting" or "pregnant." Was this another of Ceely's fantasies, or had they really been getting up to a lot more than anyone suspected? But this wasn't the time to be shocked. She had to keep the story going, trusting that her father was listening above.

"Did he get the medicine, Ceely?"

Ceely didn't answer. Her face grew angry. She suddenly turned to Tracy. "All this family trouble ain't none of your business, anyhow," she snapped.

Tracy was afraid she was about to lose the whole confession at this point. "I'm just trying to give you someone to talk to," Tracy said. "You know I didn't tell anyone about what you said last week." She hated mouthing the actual lie, but at this point, she had to.

Ceely stared at her for a long time. "I guess you didn't," she said. "But you can't tell nobody about all this."

Tracy forced a shaky smile. "I promise you, Ceely Rose, I won't be the one who tells the investigators about all this, cross my heart." She made a movement crossing her heart. That satisfied Ceely, who suddenly smiled like she didn't have a care in the world.

TABLOID CELEBRITY

Late on the day of August 12, 1896, news broke in the *Mansfield Daily Shield* that Celia Rose had been arrested for the murder of her father, mother and brother. After George Davis and his daughter Tracy revealed to Richland County prosecutor August Douglass what Ceely had said in the barn, the wheels of justice began to slowly crank. An arrest warrant was produced, and Sheriff James Boals dispatched Constable Pluck to the Ohler farm to arrest Ceely and bring her to the prosecutor's office. She was assigned lawyers, Lewis C. Mengert and James M. Reed, who advised her to be careful about what she said. She was denied bond and immediately taken to the Richland County Jail, on the square in downtown Mansfield.

Though startled at first by this strange new world, Celia quickly found that she liked certain aspects of jail. Brought in wearing a black sailor cap, Ceely took it off, sat down on the jail cot and sighed dramatically. "I have been working so hard at Mrs. Ohler's," she said. Mrs. Ohler, who had accompanied the girl into town, told a different tale, saying that the extent of the girl's labors at the farm had been to lie at length on the sofa until the dinner bell rang. Mrs. Ohler had been allowed to bring some books and sewing projects, which she gave the girl.

When she was charged, Celia pleaded not guilty to the charges against her and waived her right to a preliminary hearing. She was returned to the jail, adjoining the courthouse, to await the grand jury trial.

One thing Ceely discovered that she really enjoyed was the notoriety her crime brought her, for it resulted in numerous curious visitors at the

The Richland County Jail in Mansfield. *Bob Carter Collection.*

jail. Reporters, acquaintances and the just plain curious flocked to see her throughout the rest of August and through September as the prosecutor built his case against the young woman.

A freelancer working for the *Chicago Tribune* sketched a vivid verbal picture of the girl in jail just days after her arrest:

> *Celia Rose is in a cell in the Rutland* [sic] *County Jail in this city charged with poisoning* [her parents and brother]—*all the relatives she had in the world. She spends her time sewing, embroidering, and reading the Bible, a "Story of the Bible," and the "International Sunday-School Lesson Leaf." She shows no emotion whatever and greets visitors cheerful smile, and laughs half archly, half coquettishly at times when she is questioned about her relations to Guy Berry, the 17-year old neighbor for love of whom she is said to have confessed to a schoolgirl friend that she had caused the death of her parents and brother.*
>
> *Celia Rose has no symptoms of insanity, and while not considered bright or wholly balanced mentally, is far from being an imbecile. Nordau would class her as a degenerate. She does not appear to know the difference between right and wrong. Her moral sense, if she has any at all, is defective.*

Later in the same article:

When seen yesterday forenoon she was stretched out at full length reading the "International Sunday-School Lesson Leaf." She had on no shoes or stockings and was clad in a coarse, black woolen dress with red bands in the bodice. Her thick, neutral blond hair was done up in a neat knot, and the front curls were in papers. She did not rise when addressed, but let her pamphlet drop, and leaned forward long enough to adjust her skirt. She made no apology for her lack of shoes. They were tucked under the cot.

Miss Rose has blue eyes, straight nose, slightly thicker than usual, small and delicately shapen ears, a large, straight mouth, rosy complexion, and a finely rounded head, neck, and chin.

Her eyes are expressionless even when she laughs, which is not infrequent. Her laughter is not silly nor momentarily ill-timed. She did not laugh while one was talking about the death of her parents, but was likely to in the next breath, if she thought anything at all amusing. She talks intelligently about what she has read, but seems deficient in ideas. Her memory is retentive and her stock of facts is larger than that of the average reading woman.

The investigating officials talked extensively with the girl. Ceely outright laughed at Coroner Baughman when he asked her how the poison was administered. "I fooled you about the coffee and the poison," Ceely said gleefully. "I could have told you about the smear case sooner, but I was not ready."

On August 15, the estate sale for Rebecca Rose's property was held at the miller's cottage. People from the valley and beyond turned out in droves to get a glimpse inside the Rose family's existence. The *Chicago Tribune* freelancer realized that it would be a perfect place to get further insights.

One of the first people the reporter talked with was Tracy Davis. She recounted how she had gained Ceely's confession to the reporter and pointed out Guy Berry. Although Guy had not come to the estate sale, he was working at the Berry home and, from time to time, looked over, observing the comings and goings of people at the auction.

Tracy introduced the reporter to Guy's mother, Angeline Berry, who was in attendance. The reporter described her as "a sylph-like figure of delicate health." Mrs. Berry was indignant about some of the things Ceely had said to the press about her and Guy's relationship.

"There's not a word of truth in her statements that they were engaged," Angeline said. "She is silly on the subject of marrying and bothered Guy so much that he complained to his father and threatened to leave home unless Mr. Berry requested Mr. Rose to put a stop to the annoyance of Celia's trailing after him all the time. He does not like her. Never did. Guy has a nice sweetheart and would never have thought of marrying Celia if he had been of age, as he is not. He knew that we did not like her and he is a good son." She either took the reporter up to the Berry house to talk to her son or hailed him across the creek and had him come over to the miller's house. Guy confirmed everything his mother said and impressed the reporter, who noted, "[h]is bearing was frank and his whole demeanor inspired confidence in the truth of what he said."

The reporter returned to the auction and noted that Mrs. Rose "was evidently a thrifty housekeeper and a good provider. The larder was filled with large quantities of home-made preserves, pickles, and canned goods, apparently enough to supply the needs of a family for a year or two." Other items noted in the auction bill of sale—still on file in the Richland County Probate Court—include a box of books; numerous crocks, jugs, kettles, bottles and canning jars; numerous skillets and other pieces of kitchenware; ham, eggs, lard, flour, corn, oats, rice, potatoes, sugar, syrup and other food and spices; lanterns, lamps and candles; furniture (including Rebecca's rocking chair); a sewing machine; Rebecca's carpet loom (bought by Mrs. H.L. Charles for $3.75); six stoves (including a parlor stove that Mrs. Berry bought for $8.00); three wagons; a washing machine; miscellaneous tools; and sixty chickens, five hogs and a cow. A Eureka fanning mill, a kind of mechanical grain separator, was valued at $8.00 and bid up to $9.00 by C.F. Gladden. The biggest bidding war erupted over Rebecca's sewing machine, valued at $10.00 but bid up to $19.50 and sold to J. Charles. The total income from the estate sale was $309.31. A full listing of the sale can be found in the appendices.

The wide range of buyers at the estate sale included the Berrys, the Ohlers, the Davises, the Schracks and Phebe Herring. The elderly Mrs. Herring may have been purchasing some things on behalf of her son Clem, who couldn't directly bid on anything, as he had been appointed executor of the estate. Later, he would use a third party to purchase the house and mill property as well.

Meanwhile, examinations and questioning of Ceely continued.

An even sharper-toned tabloid article (possibly written by the same freelancer) ran in the *Saturday Globe*, a weekly newspaper published in Utica, New York, and then distributed nationally. The reason this article may well be by the same freelancer as the *Chicago Tribune* article is that this article includes photographs—something most U.S. newspapers could not yet do—that are clearly the original photographs that the illustrations in the *Tribune* article were based on. There is a photo of Ceely's brother Walter that shows him wearing a suit, tie and collar shirt, but with the typical close-cropped hair of a farmer. While not severe, his expression is not one of smiling, nor

The first of more than a dozen pages recording everything that was sold at the estate sale after Rebecca Rose's death. *Author's collection.*

does his face give the appearance of being much accustomed to smiling. He looks at an angle off to the side, not making eye contact.

There is a photograph of Tracy Davis in a stiff, high-collar dress. Her hair was either fairly short or tied in the back. While only twenty years old, Tracy comes across as older in the photo, although it must be kept in mind she'd already been out of school working for some period of time before taking on the heavy burden of drawing the confession out of her friend. It may be that the line under her eye is simply print-through from the next page of the newspaper, not an age line.

There is an illustration, apparently based on an actual family photograph of David Rose during the Civil War. Perhaps that photo was too small or too dim to be reproduced photographically and the illustration was done to show Rose in the article. It was run backward in the newspaper. The photo must have showed Rose in a uniform, holding a bayonet, which is hardly likely to have been his appearance during the war, considering that he was a miller. More likely, this was a photograph taken just before he left Latham to join the army. Photographers made a brisk business of soldier pictures, keeping quasi-

The only documented photograph of Celia Rose, which ran in the *Saturday Globe*, a national tabloid newspaper published in Utica, New York. *James Reed Collection.*

military props around for the young men to pose with. Considering that this photo once existed, it is intriguing to think that it might still be out there somewhere in the world, unless it was thrown away after the estate sale.

The single most valuable thing from this Utica tabloid article, however, is the central photograph. It is the one documented photographic image of Ceely Rose that we have. In it, she sits in a chair with a rather smug smile, clearly enjoying her own celebrity. She wears a gingham skirt and a darker blouse, with a fabric frill around the comfortable neck. Her hair is back in pigtails with a possible curl or two in front. The dark chair she sits in almost disappears into the shadow behind her, so it has been touched up to clarify the arm and back of the chair. Possible jail cell bars are dimly discernable behind her, although they seem too wide apart and may simply be additional photographic retouching.

The reporter wrote with a sense of relish:

> *The Richland county jail in this city harbors the most extraordinary criminal this state has ever known. A more fiendishly abnormal being was probably never created. The criminal is a girl of 23, flaxen-haired, pale-cheeked, large of body and brawny-limbed. The story of her crime will make strong men shiver, yet she laughs as she stutteringly tells how she killed her whole family—father, mother and brother—by administering poison to them. No man can think, without shuddering, of the tortures of arsenic poisoning—the excruciating pains of the body and the awful frenzies of the mind, the discoloration of the flesh and then death, after intense agony. But this girl saw those of her own flesh pass through these horrors and gloated over it.*

"Oh, it was fun," she said, as she described her devilish work to a girlfriend. Again she said, "I could hardly keep from laughing when mother was vomiting up that green stuff, it worked so well."

How reliable is this reporting? There is no question that the reporter is writing with one eye firmly on the potential commercial audience. In many ways, this is a prime example of the worst sort of yellow journalism that ran rampant in the late nineteenth century. The tone is sensational, and the "facts" are conflated from various sources at best and perhaps not even be true at worst.

The extracted comment about Ceely having fun with her activities may, in fact, be true, but it is taken out of its apparent original context, which was that she said this in response to Tracy's remark, "You had that fun up at the mill all by yourself." If the use of the word *fun* is horrifying when Ceely says it, it must be remembered that Tracy planted the word in her mind with that leading comment.

Laughing? It is well documented that Celia Rose had a tendency to break into laughter at the easiest provocation, so, again, the use of that to portray her as fiendish is irresponsible. It is interesting to note that in this quote, Ceely is portrayed as referring to her mother by that word, whereas elsewhere in the article, she is quoted as calling her mother "Maw." Which is it?

And "green stuff"? There is nothing about arsenic poisoning with Rough-on-Rats that would cause a green color to the victim's vomit. That seems pure sensational fiction on the reporter's part, unless it was a detail that Ceely made up on the spot. One would do well to remember that although this article provides one of our closest encounters with Celia Rose, it is through the highly distorted lens of a reporter trying to sell articles on the open market as a freelancer. This reporter is not an impartial observer.

Under the subheading "Childish Celia," the reporter continued on in like manner:

Her mother treated her with exceptional and unnecessary tenderness, because, though strong physically, the girl was mentally weak—not insane, not filled with delusions, but having a sort of mental deficiency which made her childish. She was not idiotic, for she could read, write and do examples in arithmetic and had a most retentive mind.

The article stated that Celia's only physical defect was a painful stutter that often marred her speech. It portrays Celia's confession in the following words, rendered as a direct quote:

I once heard father read in the paper about someone killing a family with rat poison. There was some rat poison in our house and I put it in an old pepper box. After paw and maw scolding me so, it made me so mad that I took the poison and went to the spring house. Then one day I took some schmeer kase which we kept there and put two spoonfuls of the poison in and mixed it well.

On the morning paw and maw and Walter got sick, I helped maw make breakfast. I got some of the schmeer kase that I fixed and put it on the table. Father ate heartily of it and so did mother and Walter. I put some on my plate, but didn't eat any. After breakfast, I put the stuff in the cupboard, but afterwards got to thinking and concluded to throw it out. I threw it in the yard.

A hen and her six chickens eat it and it killed every one of them. I buried them. I put the poison under a dock-leaf in the yard.

After paw and Walter died, mother got better and I heard Dr. Budd say to her he would now pronounce her well. The next day, mother ate a very hearty dinner and with it she had bread and milk. She told me to put the bread and milk back in the cupboard, as she would probably eat some by and by. I took about a spoonful of poison and put it in the bread and milk. About 3 o'clock mother called for it and I gave it to her. When mother ate it, she said, "Celia, this tastes kind of sweet." I didn't say anything but I was awful afraid she would detect me.

In about an hour mother got awful sick and I could hardly keep from laughing when she was vomiting up the green stuff; it worked so well. I then took the pepper box, washing it out and threw it under the same dock leaf.

The reliability of this entire passage is questionable. There may be things in it that Celia Rose actually said, although how many were by her own volition and how many were provoked by leading questions is unknowable at this point. Certainly there's an inconsistency in diction, grammar and vocabulary. Some phrases seem quite believable, while others rankle. The "vomiting green stuff" comment in particular, repeated from earlier in the article, seems off. Also, there's Ceely's supposed description of putting poison in the "bread and milk." It would be easy enough to mix a powder into milk, but not on dry bread without being obvious and being nearly impossible to handle without the carrier being made sick, too. Additionally, the supposed comment about the milk tasting "kind of sweet" lines up with no known property of either arsenic in general nor Rough-on-Rats brand poison in particular. What we appear to have here is a conflation of actual comments Ceely Rose may have made with some provoked remarks and some possible outright fabrications.

A final detail from the Utica article does have the ring of truth to it. The reporter said that at one point, Ceely said to her that she was "worried some about her folks" but that she expected to get back to the old place in a little while and everything would be all right. This comment clearly displays what some of her other odd comments and reactions hinted at: Celia Rose was unable to grasp the enormity of her crime. She still talked to her parents in dreams, so she knew they were out there somewhere. In her mind, they weren't really gone. She appears to have thought that after she established her authority and independence, everything would return to normal. She could not grasp that she would never approach normal ever again.

DR. GEORGE MITCHELL WAS brought in at the prosecutor's request to examine Celia. He immediately noted the disorder of Ceely's cell when he visited. He evidently had success drawing the girl into conversation, for Celia told him that one time, Guy Berry threw her a kiss, which she caught and kept on her cheek for two weeks. She also told him that she had talked with her parents in a dream, where her mother scolded her for what she'd done. Otherwise, she showed no remorse. Dr. Mitchell noted that in her comments about her family, Ceely showed affection for her mother, less for her brother and next to nothing for her father.

Celia kept shifting her position restlessly the whole time Dr. Mitchell interviewed her. That she didn't grasp the enormity of her situation was again demonstrated when she showed the doctor that one of the things she had done while she was sitting in jail was memorize some Bible verses for when she returned to Sunday school.

Dr. Mitchell expressed his opinion in legally damning terms. "I think she is morally deficient," Dr. Mitchell said. He did not think she was legally insane.

Prosecutor Douglass had the backing from an expert he needed. It was time to take Celia Rose to the Richland County grand jury.

THE TRIAL BEGINS

On September 7, 1896, court docket no. 241, *The State of Ohio v. Celia Rose*, came up before the grand jury. Ceely was led from the Richland County Jail up the hill to the square where the Richland County Courthouse stood. During the examination by Prosecutor Douglass, Ceely broke down and cried, but if Douglass had any fears of the girl earning the jury's sympathy, it quickly evaporated. Just seconds after crying, her reaction to something else in the courtroom made her laugh heartily. Observers noted that Ceely would make an effort to concentrate on what was being said in the courtroom but sooner or later would be distracted by something trivial that would make her smile or laugh.

In the following days, while they waited on the grand jury's determination, Drs. Finley and Erwin of Mansfield, Dr. Spenzer of Cleveland, Dr. Budd and Coroner Baughman examined Ceely Rose at the Richland County Jail. Their conclusion was that the young woman was medically and morally insane but sane by the standards of the laws of the state of Ohio. They were of the unanimous opinion that while the girl had some mental issues, she was able to distinguish between right and wrong. Prosecutor Douglass was clearly lining up his experts to lobby for conviction of murder in the first degree.

At 11:00 a.m. on Saturday, September 21, 1896, the grand jury returned three indictments against Celia Rose for murder in the first degree. Other, smaller cases were also addressed, as was a set of formal recommendations to

20. RICHLAND COUNTY COURT HOUSE, MANSFIELD, OHIO.

A vintage postcard of the Richland County Courthouse, on the square in Mansfield, Ohio. *Author's collection.*

improve conditions in the Richland County Jail. The jury visited the facility to make suggestions about furnishing cells and putting linoleum or carpet in the ladies' cells. They also recommended a door be placed at the end of the ladies' department so that the women could exercise in the corridor. They also said that the jail was "poorly lighted" and that the woodwork should be painted and the roof repaired. They also suggested fixing up the sheriff's office by purchasing him such luxuries as a desk and a safe.

One wonders how much luck they had with the notoriously tight Richland County commissioners, who were blasted in a newspaper editorial in the *Mansfield Daily Shield* on October 10 for resisting defense attorney James Reed's request for $150 to pay for an expert from the state asylum in Cleveland to travel to Mansfield and do a formal assessment of Celia's sanity. Finally, the commissioners yielded, and the defense expert was summoned.

Dr. Carpenter, of the Cleveland State Hospital, examined the young woman shortly before the trial started. Reviewing his assessment during Ceely's trial, Dr. Carpenter said that while Celia Rose was only twenty-three, she looked like she was thirty-five. While the newspaper coverage of Carpenter's testimony does not state that the doctor said anything directly, the implication is that the doctor was pointing this out to suggest that

Ceely was developmentally disabled, as patients with that diagnosis can give the appearance of being older than they actually are. If any part of her actions could be laid down to a medical condition, it would be harder to convict her.

"One should expect imbecility," the doctor said, "because of cousins, uncles, nephews." The only known nephew Ceely had was John Long. No other documentation suggests the presence of any developmental disability issues with John Long. Research contacts with a member of the Rose family have confirmed that there were other members of the family at this time with known mental health/disability issues. Dr. Carpenter added that Celia had a "strange attitude," would laugh and giggle but not look him in the eye, retreated to the corner of her jail cell and showed evidence of being untidy. Her vital signs were all normal.

SHERIFF BOALS SUBPOENAED A total of thirty-six people from which to select the jury members. Jury selection began on Monday, October 12, with twenty-seven of the thirty-six subpoenaed jurors present in front of Judge Norman Wolfe. The sheriff brought Celia Rose into the courtroom for the trial proper to begin. Prosecutor Douglass was assisted by W.H. Funke,

Lewis C. Mengert served as the assistant defense attorney for Ceely Rose and was later appointed her legal guardian by the State of Ohio. *James Reed Collection.*

while James Reed and Lewis Mengert sat with Celia at the defense table. By midafternoon, a panel of twelve jurors had been selected, sworn in and instructed. The jury, named in the newspaper coverage, comprised Clark Skiles, William Reiber, Marion Taylor, Noble Starr, Jacob Hall, William Ritchie, David Maxwell, Andrew Wood, William Denzer, Peter Benau, Julius Knoth and F.C. Voegele.

Prosecutor Douglass gave his opening statement; read the indictment against Celia Rose for murder in the first degree against her father, David Rose; and then described the murder, adding that Celia had later confessed her crime to at least twelve different people. A newspaper reporter noted that Ceely showed little interest in the proceedings except for moments when Douglass mentioned her by name, at which point she would bury her face in her handkerchief and not emerge until the prosecutor was no longer speaking about her directly.

Speaking for the defense, Lewis Mengert said that the evidence would show that Celia Rose was not responsible, and that would be their entire and sole defense. The court adjourned for the day.

Tuesday morning again saw a large number of spectators in the courtroom. The first witness called by the prosecution was Coroner George W. Baughman. At the request of the defense, other witnesses present in court who were to be called later were removed from the courtroom and placed in the jury room.

Baughman testified as to his knowledge of the Roses and identified their residence as being located 350 feet from "Sandstone school house," which must have been an alternatively used name for Valley Hall School. Baughman said that he had been summoned to the Rose farmhouse by telephone by Dr. Budd after the death of David Rose, whose body he found in the southeast room on the first floor of the Rose farmhouse, while Walter Rose continued to struggle at that time in the north room. The coroner directed Drs. Budd and Alban to conduct the postmortem and sealed the stomach and a portion of the elder Rose's bowels, as required by law. He noticed that the organs were inflamed and that there was an eruption around Rose's mouth, which was typical of the sort of burn a poison might leave. He took the organs to Drs. Erwin and Speer in Mansfield for testing. He talked with Celia that day, but not about the illness or death of her people.

On July 4, Coroner Baughman was called back to the Rose farm upon the death of Walter. He had a talk with Ceely that day about the cause of sickness, but she "could not account for it in no way." He pressured her again after her denials during the July 7 inquest but made no further progress. After the death of Rebecca Rose, Baughman accused Ceely of putting poison in the coffee she served to family members, which she again denied. He did not talk to her again until she came to the jail after confessing.

The defense objected to the witness referring to a confession. The court offered to let the defense cross-examine Baughman, but the defense insisted that the first confession had to be addressed to determine whether it was willingly given or produced under duress. The judge agreed. Coroner Baughman was dismissed for the time being, and the prosecution called Tracy Davis.

Davis was sworn in and confirmed that she lived just one mile away from the Roses and had known them for about fifteen years. She heard about the sickness that struck the Roses while she was working in Bellville, where she had been for six months. By the time she returned home, David Rose was dead. The first time she saw Ceely that spring was about three weeks after David's death, by which time Walter and Rebecca had died too. Celia came to her house, and they talked about her family's passing.

"The first time you talked to her," the prosecutor said, "what did she say about the deaths?" The defense objected, and the jury was shown out of the room while the defense cross-examined the witness. Davis said that she was the one who brought up the subject of the Rose family deaths. She asked Ceely what was the matter with them.

Davis testified that in this conversation, Celia said, "I heard it was arsenic. Rough-on-Rats," but refused to say anything more.

On July 27, Celia again walked up to the Davis home and talked with her for a bit. They kept talking as Tracy walked Ceely part of the way home. Davis said that Ceely told her people were accusing her of killing her family members but that she wouldn't tell if she had done it. Tracy told her that she must tell her because they had always been friends. Ceely said she would trust no one with it, for they'd tell on her. Davis said that she tried to get her to say more that day, but that was the extent of it. Celia said she would "study over it about a week."

The next time Tracy Davis saw Ceely Rose was at the Ohler farm. By this point, she had discussed getting Ceely's story with her father and Prosecutor Douglass. On this day, the girls took a walk to the cemetery and placed flowers on David Rose's grave. They sat down on the church steps, where Tracy told Ceely she was ready to hear the story. She said that Ceely didn't know if she could trust her.

"Did you say that your father is acquainted with Prosecutor Douglass?" one of the lawyers asked.

"No," Tracy said.

"Did you tell her that it would go easier for her if she told it?"

"She knew it would," Tracy said.

"Did you tell her that telling you would keep her out of jail?"

"I never said that." Tracy said. "I told her it would help her if she told me." Tracy Davis said that Celia Rose then proceeded to tell her in detail how she had poisoned her family.

The prosecution and defense argued about the admissibility of the confession, with Judge Wolfe deciding in favor of the prosecution. The jury was returned to the court, and Davis repeated her story of Ceely's confession.

They then proceeded to go over the details of Ceely's confession: the smear case, the rat poison, the springhouse and how Ceely initially threw out the remaining poison, causing the deaths of a hen and six chicks in the yard, which she then buried. She then put the remaining poison in a pepper box that she hid behind the house in the weeds. Tracy said that she and her sister Cora went with Ceely to the miller's house and found the tin container. They opened the box and saw a residue inside.

"There is some of it now," Celia said. "I thought I had washed it all out." She gave the tin to Tracy, who turned it over to Prosecutor Douglass.

Cross-examination clarified some details regarding when Davis had been in the valley and when she had

Judge Norman Wolfe oversaw the trial of Celia Rose. *John Sherman Room at the Mansfield/Richland County Public Library.*

been in Bellville working. In response to a defense question, Tracy said that she would describe Ceely and herself as intimate friends who confided in each other. She said that over the years they had regularly gone together to "parties and literaries." Literaries were school or church programs that featured recitations of poems and readings of stories.

Tracy said that the first time she saw Ceely after Rebecca's death, the young woman didn't talk much about her family's deaths. She did talk about Guy Berry and said that if she had a man now, she could live in the house as her father and mother were dead.

The court adjourned for lunch. On Tuesday afternoon, the cross-examination of Tracy Davis continued. She said that Ceely did not know that Tracy was coming to see her when she visited at the Ohler farm, their third conversation since the deaths of Ceely's family. She also said that she had been unaware of any tensions in the Rose family before the incidents of that spring.

Dr. Baughman was recalled. He recounted Ceely's taunting of him in jail. He said that she talked about the poison in the presence of Drs. Spenzer, Erwin, Culler, Finley, Budd and himself. Baughman said that David Rose had been dead about five or six hours when he arrived. The body was rigid with rigor mortis, and the eyes were sunken.

George Davis was called as the next witness. He described how he hid in the haymow of the Ohler barn while his daughter Tracy drew a repeat of

Ceely's confession as they sat in the buggy below. He said that she started off by saying that Guy Berry had nothing to do with what she had done, that the devil had prompted her to do it. Davis said that in addition to giving the details of how she had poisoned her family, Celia had told his daughter that she had prepared a chicken for Pastor Kramer from the church but that he didn't stop by that week. He also confirmed that Ceely referred to the Romulus Cotell murder case in Akron as the source of her idea for the entire crime.

On cross-examination, George Davis confirmed that when he first talked to the prosecutor, he inquired about the possibility of a reward. No reward was available, but he decided to go ahead because he was confident his daughter could get Celia's confession. Davis confirmed what Ceely had said about a hearse coming to bear the family away, except that he said he thought she had said it would come from Perrysville, whereas the actual undertaker, Jacob Marks, was from Lucas.

Dr. Allen Budd was called next. He confirmed that he had been the Rose family's physician for seventeen years. He went to the miller's house two days after first hearing about the sickness. He called in Dr. Culler from Lucas as a consultant on June 30. He said that David Rose's symptoms had been violent vomiting, pain in the stomach and bowels, red and excessively sore gums and constant restlessness that continued until death. He questioned Rebecca, Walter and Ceely about the possibility of poison. None of them claimed to know anything about what could have caused their situation. They discussed the possibility of poisoning caused by dyeing matter, which was apparently a household chore Rebecca had been attending to that week.

Budd helped conduct the postmortem on David Rose. He said that the stomach was normal in size but inflamed in appearance. He said he concluded at that point that arsenical poisoning was likely.

The defense asked Dr. Budd about his treatments for the Roses. Budd said that he had given them tinctures of iron and also used anodynes to relieve pain. He had given them astringents to stop diarrhea and injected morphine hypodermically for pain. He did not use a stomach pump on the victims.

First responder Dr. John McCombs was called. In addition to confirming the initial situation, he added that Celia had made herself useful in caring for her sick family members.

Perrysville physician Dr. Samuel Alban confirmed that he was not involved in the treatment of patients but had assisted in the postmortem of David Rose. He confirmed that the inflammation of Rose's stomach and upper intestines was consistent with what would be observed in arsenical poisoning.

He said that other poisons would have produced different symptoms. Prussic acid, for instance, attacks the nervous system more than the digestive system. He opined that a stomach pump would be helpful in a poison case if administered immediately. He noted that nine times out of ten, though, doctors do not carry a stomach pump with them on house calls.

Dr. John Culler of Lucas was the next consulting physician called. He had been brought in on June 30, the day David Rose died. He suspected poisoning, particularly as Walter and Rebecca's symptoms were identical to David's.

On cross-examination, it came out that no antidote for the poisoning had been given by the other physicians in the six days they had been treating the family. Dr. Culler recommended a tincture of iron be given as an antidote to probable arsenic poisoning.

Dr. Erwin of Mansfield was called to testify on the testing of David Rose's stomach and intestines. He said that he and his partner Dr. Speer found unmistakable traces of arsenic in David Rose's organs. When Prosecutor Douglass brought him the tin pepper box, Dr. Erwin tested it and found the residue of one half a grain of arsenic in it.

The defense objected to Dr. Erwin's comment on the grounds that it would lead the jury toward the alleged use of Rough-on-Rats, but the motion was overruled. Erwin said that he knew nothing about Rough-on-Rats but that he could prove through scientific testing that arsenic had been in the pepper box. The court asked him to submit the test on Wednesday.

Erwin confirmed that Coroner Baughman had delivered the entrails to him in a glass jar sealed with wax. He said that he opened Rose's stomach and found that the walls of the stomach were thickened with much inflammation. He said that strychnine would not cause inflammation as a symptom. He was asked if arsenic would cause ulceration, but he said that it typically would not—that it was an irritant, but not a caustic. Asked about the similarity of symptoms between arsenic poisoning and cholera morbus, Dr. Erwin said that cholera does not produce the same burning stomach pains as arsenic.

ON THE THIRD DAY of the trial, attendance was down, due to races being held at the fairgrounds. Constable Pluck, who had been sworn in at the end of the second day, was examined in more detail Wednesday morning. Pluck testified that he had accompanied the prosecutor and Miss Davis to the Richland County Jail to meet with Celia Rose. Douglass asked Celia about the details of what she did and why she did it but paused to inform her of her right to not answer, as anything she said could be used against her in court. He had Tracy Davis confront Ceely with what she had previously said. Ceely confirmed it.

Jane Ohler was called to the stand next. She said that she had known the Roses for many years. She said that she did not hear about the sickness in the family until the Sunday after it happened. She went to the miller's house that evening to check in on the family. After Rebecca's death, Celia came to live with the Ohlers, where she resided for the next eighteen days until she was arrested.

Early on, the Ohlers had been outspoken in their belief in Ceely's innocence. It seems that this belief began to crumble during the time Ceely was present in their home. Mrs. Ohler said that she had heard rumors about Ceely confessing. She asked Ceely at one point if she thought that anyone had seen her put anything in the family's victuals that day. Ceely did not answer.

The state called George Berry, Guy Berry's father. He confirmed that on June 4, he had gone to the mill to speak with David Rose about Celia pestering his boys. Later, when he heard about the poisoning the morning of June 24, he headed over to the miller's cottage around noon and found the family sick. When he returned the following morning, he noticed in the Roses' fenced yard a number of dead chickens.

After Tracy Davis and her father were each recalled to clarify some details, the state rested its case, with the understanding that it reserved the right to reopen its prosecution if it was able to get expert witness Dr. Spenzer of the Newburgh State Hospital to arrive in time for the trial.

The defense's first witness was Reverend W.H. Dolbeer of Lucas. Dolbeer was of the opinion that Celia Rose could be taught not to do specific things but lacked the ability to make those connections herself. He said that the girl was not of sound mind from when he first saw her, but she was not a raving maniac. He admitted that if she could steal a book (which she did, from Clem Herring), that she had cunning, and that if she knew it was wrong to steal a book, she might know it was wrong to commit murder. He was not convinced, however, that Celia was able to make that judgment.

Court then adjourned for the day.

THE DEFENSE GATHERS STEAM

Attendance was back up on Thursday as the defense's case gathered steam.

Ceely's schoolmate Lavina Andrews was called. Lavina's family lived in the farm at the top of the valley wall directly behind Valley Hall School. She testified that Celia visited her home about once per month. About six years ago, Lavina had been with Ceely in school, where she said that Ceely was in the class with nine- or ten-year-olds even though Ceely herself was seventeen. When she played, it was with the younger children. When she didn't play, she watched the boys play ball. She said that Ceely had learned to sew but could not crochet. She added that the girl was not a good reader and never got further in math than long division.

Sensing the direction of the defense's portrayal of Ceely's mental faculties, Prosecutor Douglass on cross-examination asked the witness if she thought that inability to crochet indicated insanity, no doubt drawing hearty laughs from the spectators in the courtroom. Andrews admitted that it did not.

One of Celia's former schoolteachers, Eva Tucker, was called next to the stand. Tucker taught at Valley Hall School in the winter of 1893–94. One time she assigned Ceely to do a recitation of a humorous poem. The one she selected was twenty-four lines long, and the girl could only recite it by holding up the paper in front of her face so that she couldn't see her schoolmates. Tucker said that she considered Celia Rose silly, not of sound mind.

The prosecution asked Tucker if she thought that Ceely knew the difference between right and wrong. Tucker said that she thought that Ceely would if she were specifically taught about something. Tucker said that she did not believe Celia Rose understood the enormity of the crimes she had committed. The prosecutor asked if Ceely's behavior made her obviously stand out from other students.

"She does not act like other people," Tucker said. When pressed by the prosecutor to say if she was surprised by Ceely's crime, the teacher admitted she was. She said she never thought Ceely would commit murder until she did it and that she would have been just as surprised to hear of any other girl she taught doing it.

Celia's most recent teacher, Emma Halderman, was next. Halderman had taught at Valley Hall School during the spring term of 1895. She said that Ceely had come to the school four or five times to be involved in literary performances on Fridays. One time, she was assigned to memorize a very short recitation from a Lutheran leaflet. Halderman said that Ceely's manner was peculiar. "She stammered and I prompted her," Halderman said. "It increased her embarrassment. She was very nervous."

Another time, the teacher had Ceely do a reading of "Buckwheat Cake and Molasses," which went a little better because the girl could read. On one occasion, when Ceely hadn't been to school in a while, she saw the teacher at Marion Schrack's house and got excited when the teacher invited her to visit school again.

"The little girls won't know me!" Ceely said, clapping her hands in excitement. She was very disappointed when she got to school and found that the little children remembered her perfectly well. Halderman said she had no idea why Ceely would have thought the children wouldn't know her.

The prosecution sparred a little with Halderman on cross-examination, evaluating how many lines Ceely was capable of memorizing and what sort of pieces she was given. Halderman evidently disagreed with the prosecution that the problem lay in the pieces she had given Ceely. "The trouble with her is that she is weak-minded," Halderman said. The prosecution had no further questions of the witness.

After a short recess for lunch, the prosecution asked to reopen direct examination. Its key witness, Dr. John Spenzer of Cleveland, had finally made it to Mansfield. Spenzer was a medical chemist and toxicologist who had begun his studies in 1874 and had received training in France, Germany, Switzerland and in the United States. He received internal organs to study for the determination of metallic poisonings. He read out his report on his examination of Walter Rose's entrails. It said that he found arsenic beyond a reasonable question of doubt in Rose's stomach, liver and kidney.

When Dr. Spenzer tested Rebecca Rose's organs, he found higher levels of arsenic than he'd seen in either David or Walter's tests, suggesting that she had been poisoned a second time, quickly causing her death. The early poisoning had caused David and Walter's deaths, but it took several days, allowing the arsenic to begin depleting from their bodies.

Asked for details of his testing procedure, Dr. Spenzer explained, "I took a position of the viscera, and decomposed it by acid. After this was done, I filtered it past hydrogen sulfide. Precipitate was yellow, giving a hint of arsenic. The precipitate was washed and arsenious acid was found, which was changed to arsenic acid." Test tubes of the arsenic remnants recovered from the Roses' organs were introduced into evidence.

The defense reopened with Dr. E.G. Carpenter, a brain disease specialist who worked at the Newburgh State Hospital for the Insane in Cleveland. He talked about confirmed cases of mental illness elsewhere in the Rose family, although the newspaper reports of the trial that survive do not name names.

"In a person having cousins, uncles, and nephews imbecilic, one should expect to find an idiot," Dr. Carpenter said. He said that although Celia Rose was twenty-three, her appearance was more like a woman of thirty-five. He said that this was a typical symptom of imbecility. The doctor said that when he examined Ceely, her manner was strange. She wouldn't look him in the eye and would often laugh and giggle, while keeping to the untidy corner of her jail cell. He said that the deaths of her family did not seem to affect her much. He concluded that Celia had deficient mental development.

Anticipating the prosecution's coming angle, the defense attorneys asked Dr. Carpenter if it were possible for a person to both be an imbecile and have cunning. Carpenter said it was absolutely possible, that an idiot in some cases can be phenomenally bright in a few select areas, while deficient elsewhere.

The prosecution's cross-examination of Dr. Carpenter delved into details of an imbecile's potential level of moral insanity. Carpenter said that he thought Celia Rose could be taught to some degree, but not enough to ensure that she'd understand the seriousness of her crimes. He said that when he talked with her, he asked Ceely at one point why she killed her mother and father.

"I wanted to be the boss in my own house," Celia said.

Another neighbor of the Roses, Amanda Andrews, was called next by the defense. She, too, said that she had never considered Celia Rose "right," but on cross-examination, she said that she thought the girl was bright enough to know that murder was wrong. Finding a little bit of traction with Andrews, the prosecutor asked if she thought that in a situation where Ceely might be confronted with something she'd never been taught about—such as, say burning down a house—that Ceely would be able to tell that this action would be wrong.

"I believe so," Mrs. Andrews said.

On re-direct examination, the defense countered this damage by asking Mrs. Andrews to tell the jury about a visit she had made to the Rose home. On that occasion, Andrews had heard Celia carrying on a conversation with herself.

Mrs. Willard Darling was called next. She was Ceely's teacher when the girl was twelve. She said that Ceely regularly attended school that year but lagged four to six years behind other students her age. Mrs. Darling said that Celia always played with younger children and in the manner of a younger child. She said that she believed the girl to be weak-minded, an imbecile.

On cross-examination, Darling refused to comment on whether she thought that Ceely would know that murder was wrong, saying only that she believed the girl had a limited idea of right and wrong. She said that she had seen Ceely once slap a younger child in a fit of anger. The prosecution tried to play that down, asking her if in fifteen years of teaching, she had never seen an older boy slap a younger one. Darling said she had not. Regarding Celia's level of achievement, the prosecutor asked Darling if she knew for certain that Ceely had attended school at all previous to that year. Darling admitted that she had no knowledge of that.

Jane Ohler, who had earlier appeared as a prosecution witness, was called by the defense. She described Celia's stay at her house, where she played a lot with the Ohlers' smallest children and worked but little. Ohler opined that Celia Rose would never be able to earn a livelihood on her own.

Dr. William Bushnell of Mansfield testified about his examination of the defendant. Over the course of several conversations with her, the doctor came to the conclusion that Celia Rose was of an incompetent mind. He said that in cases of imbecility, the person's willpower is diminished. Bushnell said on cross-examination that Celia might know that burning a building down or committing a murder was wrong, but due to her condition, she would not have the willpower to resist doing it, if that was what she wanted. He said that while she was not a raving maniac presently, she had the potential to become one.

Lavina Andrews's sister Alti testified next, likewise saying that she thought Celia insane.

Dr. A.H. McCullough of Mansfield testified that he had examined and conversed with Celia Rose. He concluded that she was not of sound mind, that she was an imbecile with a mind not fully developed. He said that her higher faculties were not developed, like a child. He believed her insane.

On cross-examination, Dr. McCullough said that he did not feel that Celia Rose was capable of distinguishing between right and wrong. Asked if he thought Ceely would know it was wrong to, say, plunge a dagger into a playmate, he said he didn't think she would. Asked if he thought that weak-minded people should be held responsible for their acts, the doctor said yes. He said that during his examination, Ceely told him of a dream she'd had in which her mother told her that if she did the poisoning, she would go to the penitentiary and not be admitted to heaven.

After a lunch break, during testimony by John Ohler, the defense seized on Ohler's reference to mental issues in the Rose family to bring the prosecutor himself to the stand, as he is evidently where Ohler first heard of these other issues of mental illness.

Augustus Douglass was sworn in and questioned. He confirmed that it was known that David Rose was the brother of Virgil D. Rose and Mrs. Martha Barrett of Highland County and that Mrs. Barrett was the mother of the two weak-minded children whom had been mentioned earlier in the trial. It was a coup for attorneys Reed and Mengert to have this information testified to by the prosecuting attorney himself.

The defense returned to Mr. Ohler. He said that at one point after the deaths of the Roses, he was driving Ceely past the Pleasant Valley Cemetery. He was asking her some questions about the deaths, but Ceely wasn't being responsive. A rabbit suddenly darted among the gravestones, grabbing Ceely's attention, and she dropped the subject of the loss of her family completely. Ohler said that Ceely behaved the same in church as she did everywhere else. He said that he believed her insane. Asked about Ceely's ability to judge during cross-examination, Ohler said he didn't think she had any moral thought. He said she knows wrong from right but doesn't appreciate the enormity of her crimes.

Fifteen-year-old Flora Schrack, who decades later would write a memoir of the case, was sworn in as the next defense witness. She talked about Ceely at school, playing with children, clapping her hands and dancing in excitement while watching the boys play baseball.

Dr. W.E. Loughridge testified about examining Ceely. He said that she presented an appearance much older than she actually was. He said that she frowned, giggled and stammered extensively. Questioned as to her residence,

Celia described the farm, its location and who had been living there. Ceely said she had a play house. Her mother had spent some time there with her. She also said that she had cooked in her play house, but the ingredients were sand. Loughridge gave her sums to compute, which she was able to do. He said she remembered dates with unusual accuracy. He said she claimed that she didn't feel well at her father's funeral due to rheumatism.

Loughridge said that he got the impression that Ceely resented her father's opposition but that she had no ill feeling toward her mother or brother. When she put poison in the smear case, she simply wanted to poison her father. The doctor also said that Ceely told him she didn't see any reason why one person could not kill another. He believed her insane.

On cross-examination, Dr. Loughridge allowed that Celia Rose possessed cunning and that he couldn't rule out the possibility that she could have been deceiving him, although he added that insanity is extremely difficult to fake. Dr. Loughridge disagreed with some of the other doctors about her diagnosis as an idiot. "Celia Rose has a weak mind," Loughridge said, "but a degree of development not known to an idiot."

The defense's next witness was Aurelius Tucker, who lived across the road from the Ohler farm (which he owned and rented to the Ohlers until they purchased the land in 1897). Tucker told the story of the time Rebecca Rose and her daughter stopped by to visit. Ceely was fascinated with the Tuckers' new wallpaper in their living room, which had a pattern of roses. Ceely went from rose to rose, kissing each one throughout the large room. Tucker said that he had known the Roses since they moved to Pleasant Valley and that he judged Celia Rose to be an imbecile of unsound mind.

Elmer Cunning had taught Ceely in 1883, 1890 and 1891. He testified that she had no ability to learn and that he believed her to be insane. The prosecution pushed Cunning on his estimation of Ceely's mental abilities, but he insisted that he'd been unable to make any impression on her as a teacher. He had on other occasions seen her at public events, and these situations did nothing to change his opinion.

"She acted silly," Cunning said, "just as she's doing now." The reporter did not record what Ceely was doing in the courtroom that prompted Cunning's comment. Cunning was the teacher on duty on the day Ceely got lost during the heavy rain, and the defense opened a re-direct examination of Cunning to have him tell that story to the court.

Valley Hall School teacher and Justice of the Peace John Tucker was up next. He had led classes at the school in 1886 and 1887. He said that Celia never got out of the second reader and was schooled with children younger than herself. When she was thirteen, she was being taught with the six- to ten-year-olds. He said that he believed the girl to be weak-minded. On cross-examination, he said that he thought she might understand the difference between right and wrong but wouldn't appreciate the enormity of the crime.

Eighteen-year-old Maud Schrack was the next defense witness, someone who had known Celia for eleven years and saw her on average once a week. She talked of some of the peculiar things Ceely would do, such as jumping out from behind a door to try to scare Maud. She said that Ceely had done this as recently as that spring.

Gus Douglass had a field day with Maud's testimony. On cross-examination, he made the teenage girl step down from the stand and reenact how Ceely would jump out from behind a door to try to scare her. After she performed this, Douglass asked her if she thought that this action proved Celia Rose was insane. Schrack fumbled her answer, saying it seemed a little odd for a twenty-three-year-old to do that.

Douglass then sprang his little trap. "That's funny," he said. "I've jumped out from behind doors to scare people, yet no one has ever accused me of insanity." The courtroom roared in laughter, and when Schrack's sister wrote a recollection of the case almost seventy-five years later, she said that Maud never forgave Douglass for ridiculing her in court, in front of spectators.

But the move was a mark of the prosecution's growing desperation, as witness after witness testified that he or she thought Celia Rose had serious mental problems and had so for years. Since her crimes involved poison, Ceely's prosecutors had to convince the jury that she was of sound enough mind to be responsible for her actions. Anything less than that would result in a verdict of not guilty by reason of insanity. Their witness Dr. Spenzer had impressed with his medical knowledge. If the local doctors had been less impressive with the revelation that they didn't begin an iron treatment as an antidote to the arsenic until several days after the poisoning, they were at least compelling eyewitnesses to the awfulness of the Roses' symptoms. But the defense was finding a seemingly endless stream of people from Pleasant Valley willing to testify that they had long thought Ceely Rose was a bit "off."

Twenty-eight-year-old Minnie Andrews gave a deposition about her knowledge of the Rose family, whom she had known for sixteen years. She taught school in 1893 and had Celia Rose as a student. Andrews said that the girl was not nearly as advanced as other scholars. At that time, Ceely was twenty, and Andrews estimated her intellectual level to be about that of a ten-year-old, but she often acted like a six-year-old, giggling, laughing and so on. Andrews said she did not believe the girl to be sane.

On cross-examination, the prosecution asked Andrews her estimation of Ceely's parents' level of education. Andrews said that Mr. and Mrs. Rose were not well educated. Queried about Ceely's level of understanding and what she might have been taught by her parents, Andrews said that she thought Ceely did not understand crime and that the balance of the family was not very bright either, although she often heard the mother correct Ceely.

Dr. George Mitchell was called to the stand next. The Mansfield doctor shared his impressions of talking with Ceely and of her appearance of disorder. He told how Ceely said that Guy had thrown a kiss to her, which she caught and kept on her cheek for two weeks, as well as how she was working on memorizing some Bible verses to give when she returned home to Sunday school after the trial. She recited part of the Ten Commandments and claimed that she knew what "Thou shalt not kill" meant.

Dr. R.S. Boles testified about treating the family over the years, including once treating Celia for diphtheria. He talked about her peculiar manner, giggling, tittering and laughing. He believed she was an imbecile and was insane. Upon cross-examination, Dr. Boles stated that there was a difference between the diagnosis of idiocy or imbecility. He said that an imbecile was one born without any particular trouble but who fails to develop normally. An idiot was born with no possibility of normal development. While Boles adjudged Ceely an imbecile, he said that this was still a form of insanity.

After a short conference, the defense rested its case at this point, turning things back over to the prosecution, which had hustled to produce more witnesses.

Pleasant Valley farmer Marion Schrack testified that he'd had ample opportunities to observe Celia Rose during her visits to his home to see his daughters. He felt that while Ceely was foolish and rather silly, she was bright in other aspects. He felt she could distinguish between right and wrong, despite not being of sound mind.

Seeing that Gus Douglass had lined up a slew of new witnesses to back up his interpretation of the case, the defense quietly but devastatingly honed in on what could undermine the first new witness's credibility.

"Mister Schrack, are you any relation to Prosecutor Douglass?" Schrack confirmed that he was a cousin of Gus Douglass. Although several others would testify to their belief that Ceely Rose was of sound mind, the defense had planted a seed inferring that Douglass had such a weak case that he had to appeal to relatives to back him up in court. It was a strong blow against the prosecution that lingered.

Neighbor Phebe Herring testified next. Having known the Roses for many years and having had Celia Rose in her house many times, Herring felt that she was well positioned to comment.

"She is not insane by any means," Mrs. Herring said. She pointed out that Ceely knew it was the right thing when she joined the Pleasant Valley Lutheran Church. On cross-examination, though, she admitted that Ceely's mother might have had something to do with that. She did know, however, that Celia had committed a crime at least once before. She told the story of Ceely stealing a package from the Herring mailbox that contained a book. When questioned, she denied it, but she confessed when the book was found in her possession.

Lorain Wolfe, who lived near the Roses, testified that she had known Ceely for some years, seeing her at school gatherings, at church and at Sunday school. She said that Ceely wasn't of sound mind but that she wasn't insane. "Her mind isn't as sound as other people," Wolfe said. "But it's not very far below ordinary people."

At this juncture, the court adjourned until Friday.

CLOSING AND VERDICT

Court convened for the fifth day of the trial at 8:35 a.m., Friday, October 16. George Davis was brought back by the state for a rebuttal. He said that not only did he believe Celia Rose knew the difference between right and wrong, but he had also heard her questioned before on that very subject and felt that it proved she understood the distinction.

Rose neighbor Tilman Wiles testified that he had seen Celia Rose enough over the years to form an opinion about her mental capacity. He said that he believed her to be sane and that she knew right from wrong. Wiles said that as a customer of the mill, he had been to the Rose house and mill many times and had spoken directly to Ceely one time when the mill was closed to find out why. "I never thought Celia Rose was weak-minded," Wiles said. "I thought her in a great measure to be as sane as other girls."

George Berry was brought back to testify about how he first told David Rose that Ceely was chasing after his boys. He said that he believed it was not the act of a sound mind but that he had observed enough of Celia over the years to make him think she could distinguish right from wrong.

Coroner Baughman was returned to the stand to finish his testimony from earlier in the trial. He testified that he had examined Celia Rose and come to the conclusion that she was medically insane and morally insane but, by the standards of the law, sane. He cited medical texts that defined the differences between medical and legal insanity. On cross-examination, he clarified that a person with any degree of insanity—imbecility, mania, chorea, lunacy, moral and more—would be defined as medically insane. A morally insane person has all faculties but the moral. A legally insane person is one who is not amenable to law.

When the defense asked Dr. Baughman if the prosecutor had instructed him what to say, he hotly denied it and gave his medical opinion of her diagnosis. "She is an imbecile, not an idiot," Baughman said. "An idiot is one who is born weak-minded, totally lacking in reasoning powers, and is not susceptible to education. Imbecility is due to weakening of physical powers and mental powers." The defense did not ask, and he did not go into detail about how Celia Rose could have potentially "weakened."

Dr. Allen W. Budd of Perrysville was recalled to the stand. He testified that he had tended the Rose family at least once a year for the last sixteen years, with a particularly busy stretch in 1880 and 1881, when he visited multiple times, treating Celia for malarial fever. He had had many chances to talk with her and instructed her on how to care for sick family members, which he said she did very well. "I never regarded her as insane," Dr. Budd said. "I regarded her as silly."

Of all the doctors who testified in the trial, it was the next one who was to deliver the loaded term that would color the public's perception of Celia Rose forever after. Dr. Samuel Alban started off with the usual description of examinations and conversations that led him to think that she was weak-minded but not insane.

"She is not intellectually insane, she is emotionally insane," Dr. Alban said. He then quietly dropped the bombshell no one else had dared verbalize: "She is a sexual pervert." He said that if Celia Rose committed the crime, it was because she thought her people stood in the way of her gratification. This labeling of Ceely as a "sexual pervert" put her obsession with Guy Berry in a dramatic light. Perhaps Dr. Alban thought that this would ensure her conviction. If he did, he was mistaken.

On cross-examination, Dr. Alban said that he would not diagnose Celia Rose as either an imbecile or an idiot. He next said something that appears to allude to his label for Ceely. "Natural causes may lead to emotional insanity, and may be cultivated afterwards. Mental weakness generally follows." It appears that he was trying to connect Ceely's case to that great bugaboo of nineteenth-century health: masturbation. It sounds as if he was politely attempting to portray Celia Rose as a normal enough girl to start with, who had a weakness for sexual arousal and subsequently masturbated herself into weak-mindedness. By modern medical standards, this belief is nonsense, although it was widely held at the time.

Dr. Mary J. Finley of Mansfield testified that she had examined Celia Rose and regarded her as an imbecile who was mentally and morally weak-minded, that she was not an idiot and that she was educable enough to know the difference between right and wrong. Dr. John Culler of Lucas followed, with essentially the same conclusions.

Pleasant Valley resident Wesley McDermott was called to the stand next. He said that the Roses had been to his house a number of times over the years, although he had never visited them. He said that he believed Celia Rose was capable of knowing the difference between right and wrong, that she would know it was wrong to burn down a building.

The defense challenged McDermott's estimation of the girl. Asked how many times he had actually had a direct conversation with Celia Rose, McDermott said it was about six times, plus he had listened to her speak at the coroner's inquest at the school. Asked if he felt Ceely was not completely mentally together, he had an answer. "No worse than the balance of the Rose family." Asked if he had expressed any thoughts about handling her case in some manner other than a trial, McDermott answered that earlier on, saying that they could save the county some expense by "mobbing her." This can only be taken to mean he threatened to lynch the girl. The defense had no further questions.

Dr. Erwin was brought up next for the state. He said that while he believed that Celia Rose was defective in the higher mental functions, she did indeed know the difference between right and wrong. On cross-examination, the defense asked Dr. Erwin if mental illness was one of his specialties as a doctor. He said it was not.

The prosecution had found a former teacher of Ceely's who thought that the girl was sane. Her name was Mary Switzer, and she was called next. She testified that she taught at the Valley Hall School in 1890 and 1891. She said that while Celia's mind may be defective, she believed the girl was sane and knew the difference between right and wrong.

The prosecution called up Jerry Tucker and his wife, as well as Mattie Wolfe, all Pleasant Valley residents, all of whom said Ceely was weak-minded but capable of distinguishing between right and wrong. The state rested its case, and the defense had no further witnesses. Judge Wolfe adjourned the court for the day and directed counsel to prepare to deliver their closing arguments Monday.

Reporting on the final day of the trial, the reporter from the *Daily Shield* described the defendant's manner: "The demeanor of the girl, Celia Rose, throughout the entire trial has been one of careless indifference to what was being done. She seemed to think it was all an entertainment gotten up in her honor, that all her friends and neighbors in Monroe township might come and see her. Her face has worn the habitual smile of a timid, bashful school girl. All reference to her mental condition did not seem to cause any lively interest although she would at times listen very attentively to a witness for a time until her attention would be diverted by some trivial happening, when she would at once pay attention to the latter."

He added that when he interviewed Ceely in the county jail, he was able to make no progress with her until he started talking about Guy Berry. The reporter added that she was smart enough to not say anything about the poisonings, saying that her lawyers told her not to talk about it. He then let slip a little of the mechanics of yellow journalism of that time: he said that Ceely was also smart enough to figure out that he was in disguise when he visited her in jail. He had claimed that he was a member of a family from the valley whom she hadn't seen in a long time, but she quickly saw through that.

"I'm not going to say anything to you," Ceely said.

"Why?" the reporter asked.

"Cause you might put it in the paper," she said.

The reporter also said that it was a matter of much discussion that Guy Berry was never put on the stand. Digging into it, the reporter found that Berry had indeed been subpoenaed, but the lawyers in the end decided not to put him on the spot. The reporter also talked about the sensation Dr. Alban had created with his "unfortunate" use of the word *pervert*. He said the doctor possibly understood the mental condition of the girl but deplored his use of a word that had a more sensational common meaning to the general public than its medical usage had at that time.

But the reporter acknowledged the powerful interpretation the doctor had presented. "He described the girl as a sexual pervert," the reporter wrote, "and that her inclinations in that line would be so strong that even human life would be sacrificed if it stood between the girl and the gratification of her desires."

The newspaper also ran an editorial defending the expense of the trial, stating that it was a necessary exercise since the defendant's life was at stake. Not all papers were supportive though. The *Butler Enterprise* ran an editorial saying that debate about the case was causing considerable wrath. It noted that the appointed lawyers Mengert (Democrat), Reed (Republican) and

Funke (Prohibitionist) were paid $300 each for their services. "It seems to have required the combined talent of three political parties to have Celia adjudged insane," the editorial mocked. "There not being any Populist lawyer at the bar, Celia did not have the benefit of that political organization."

ON MONDAY, WILLIAM FUNKE opened the prosecution's closing argument, and then Lewis Mengert spoke for the defense. James Reed closed the defense's statement, and Augustus Douglass wrapped up the state's case.

What resonated the most in spectators' memories was defense attorney James M. Reed's closing:

[I]*t is one of the characteristics of insane persons to be cunning and subtle. They say an insane person can reason to some extent, but that his power to reason correctly depends upon the degree of his insanity. The difficulty with an insane person is that he reasons insanely, and because he reasons insanely, he arrives at absurd and terrible conclusions. He acts insanely, and for that reason his acts are necessarily violent. Insane persons and imbeciles have passions. In fact, some of their passions become stronger after they become insane. While the will power which controls the passion becomes so weakened by disease that it cannot control and govern their abnormally developed passions, and that is when deeds of violence take place, and this is the period when a person is no longer responsible for his acts. They may know the act is wrong but they cannot avoid doing it.*

James M. Reed served as principal defense attorney for Celia Rose. *James Reed Collection.*

It was a shrewd closing on Reed's part, arguing Celia Rose's essential insanity but also pulling in, by implication, the arguments of the state's most sensational witness, Dr. Alban, in support of its insanity defense.

The closing arguments took the entire day. On Tuesday morning, October 20, 1896, Judge Wolfe instructed the jury and sent it into deliberations at 9:00 a.m. An hour and a half later, the jury returned with a verdict of not guilty by reason of insanity.

The prosecution declined to prosecute the remaining charges against Celia Rose but refused to nolle them. At the prosecution's request, Celia Rose was to be sent to the Toledo State Hospital for the Insane.

ASYLA

Even in 1896, it took some time to process paperwork and make arrangements. Defense attorney Lewis C. Mengert was appointed Celia Rose's legal guardian by the State of Ohio on December 12, providing someone to sign off on the paperwork to commit Ceely to the asylum. Sheriff James Boals escorted her out of the Richland County Jail and into a carriage on December 17. He accompanied her to the Toledo State Hospital, where she was signed into the institution's admissions book as patient no. 1937.

The Toledo State Hospital was part of the state system of lunatic asylums distributed throughout the state. In the late 1800s, Richland County mental patients were committed to the Toledo facility, which remained the case until a newer hospital opened in Lima in 1915. The asylum in Toledo had been built in 1888, designed by architect Edward O. Fallis. It was designed in the progressive manner of the day, on what was termed the "cottage plan," housing patients in numerous small dorms and only putting the most severely disturbed patients in larger group dorms. Fallis designed the complex in an attractive Flemish baroque style, with several lagoons on the landscaped grounds, which made the hospital an attractive picnic location around the turn of the century. After the phasing out of the state hospital system in Ohio, the entire complex was demolished in the 1970s.

It is not known exactly where Celia Rose was housed at the Toledo facility. One vintage postcard identifies an ornate building as "the female dorm," but with a total of thirty-two separate dorm buildings on the campus, there is no guarantee that Ceely was housed there.

Above: A vintage postcard of the administration building of the Toledo State Hospital. *Author's collection.*

Opposite: A vintage postcard of the landscaped grounds and lagoons at the Toledo State Hospital. *Author's collection.*

Indeed, precious little is known of Ceely's time in the state hospitals. But to fully tell that story, I must depart from our historical narrative to explain some of the maneuvering it takes to research a case like this. Hoping to find some trace of records for Ceely's institutionalization, I contacted state officials. I was told that most old records from the state hospitals had been destroyed. I asked if any records at all survived from Toledo. The woman I spoke with said that, yes, a small group of records did remain from Toledo, but it was unlikely the patient I was searching for would be in them. I said, "But the search could be done, correct?" She said, "It could be done, but we aren't likely to find anything." "But," I said, getting irritated, "you can, in fact, do the search I'm requesting, yes?" The woman sighed and said, yes, they could do the search, even though it was extremely unlikely there would be anything.

A week later, I got a call back from the state. The woman was quite perky and said that she was amazed: they actually found something. She said that it was only a few things, but it was indeed for the patient I was researching.

"Great!" I said. "Can you send them to me?"

"No," the woman replied. "Mental patient records can only be released to the nearest surviving kin. Are you related to Celia Rose?"

"No," I said. "I'm a historical researcher. You mean to tell me that even after all these years, these records are not available to historians?"

Toledo State Hospital Lagoon, Toledo, Ohio.

"That is correct," she said.

"But you can release them to the patient's nearest surviving relative?" I said.

"Yes," she said.

"Great," I said. "I'll have him call you."

In my process of researching the case, I had come into contact with a genealogical researcher named Jerry Pearson of Chillicothe, Ohio, who was attempting to untangle the knot of Rose family trees in southern Ohio, as he was descended from a Rose. Another genealogical researcher put me in contact with Jerry, and I immediately asked if his Roses were the same as the ones I was researching. I noted that we both showed a David Rose.

Jerry responded promptly but not encouragingly, citing that there were at least three known David Roses who lived in Pike County, Ohio, around the time of the Civil War.

I said that "mine" was the father of Ceely Rose, the notorious poisoner of Pleasant Valley, who had wiped out her entire family with rat poison mixed in their food.

"That's an amazing story," Jerry e-mailed. "But not my family. I've never heard of anything like that." But as a final confirmation, he sent me the dates of "his" David Rose. It was the same person.

What Jerry and I were slowly able to piece together was that we were indeed working on the same family. The almost unimaginable trauma these murders, the trial and publicity must have had caused evidently led to an unusual course. The Rose and Easter families of southern Ohio had

A vintage postcard of a female dorm at the Toledo State Hospital. *Author's collection.*

conferred and made a big decision: They were never going to speak of Celia Rose ever again, so that the younger generations would never have to know that a murderer in their own family had once obliterated an entire branch of the tree. The vow of silence had lasted for more than a century.

Jerry was floored once he realized beyond a doubt that we were talking about the same family. "Um, sorry to break the news," I said.

"It's all right," Jerry said. "I come from the sane side of the family. You shake the family tree hard enough, some nuts are going to fall out." Jerry was able to confirm the incidence of other mental health issues in the family. He was particularly intrigued by the trial testimony that referred to David Rose's sister as having two mentally infirm children. David's younger sister, Martha Jane, was Jerry's great-great-grandmother. According to him, she lived in Latham when she married John Wesley Davis, later moving to Highland County and marrying Joseph Barrett. This matched her name with the name of David Rose's sister given in trial testimony. Additional proof was provided by Jerry, who said that Martha had her brother David listed by his June 2, 1829 birthdate in her diary, although she had never been able to bring herself to write in his death date, even though she lived until 1907.

Jerry said that while he wasn't aware of Martha Jane having two children with mental problems, he was able to trace down one, William A. Barrett, who apparently never left home. The 1900 census for Brush Creek, Highland

County, shows William, age twenty-seven, living at home. No occupation is given for him, which seems significant. He appears to be the same William A. Barrett later listed as a patient at the Ohio Hospital for Epileptics in Gallipolis, Ohio, on a World War I draft card. His nearest relative is listed in extremely sloppy handwriting as (possibly) "James B. Leety" of Greenfield, Ohio, or at least that was how the record was transcribed into online digital databases. Greenfield straddles the border of Highland and Ross Counties, which is certainly home territory for the Rose family, but there is no James B. "Leety" to be found there, in any period. There is, however, a James B. Setty, who, it turns out, was the husband of William A. Barrett's half sister, Elizabeth Jane Davis. And it also turns out that Greenfield is less than five miles away from South Salem, Ohio, where Ceely's nephew John Long was living in 1896. Finally, the threads were beginning to tie everything together.

Jerry Pearson said that the impression he had received of Martha Jane (Rose) Barrett was that she was a very sad and isolated woman who may well have herself suffered from a mental health condition such as severe depression or bipolar disorder. These pieces of information confirm the testimony about mental issues in the Rose family.

Since the state would not release Celia Rose's few surviving records to me, I had Jerry contact the department. It sent the records to him, and he immediately copied me on the spotty documents. The female patient register describes Celia Rose by filling in a very few of the blanks on the form:

No.: 1937
Name: Celia Rose
Age: 23
County: Richland
Date of Admission—Month: Dec., Day: 17, Year: 1896
Civil Condition: 5
No. of Children:
Age of Youngest:
Nativity: Ohio
Degree of Education: Com.
Habits of Life: Good
Religious Persuasion:
Color of Hair: Light
Color of Eyes: Blue
Height—Ft: 5, In: 8
Weight: 155

Age at 1ˢᵗ Attack: 23
Number of Previous Attacks and Duration of Each:
Duration of Present Attack:
Readmission:
Accompanying Bodily Diseases on Admission:
Apparent or Alleged Causes—Predisposing Causes—Insane Relatives:
Other: Heredity
Exciting: Congenital
Form of Mental Order: Imbecile
Particular Propensities: Homicidal
Affectations of Sense & Intellect:

That was all expected information. What wasn't expected was the next piece of data:

Date of Discharge—Month: Nov, Day: 10, Year: 1897
Time in Asylum—Years: Mos: 10, Days: 13
Cause of Discharge: Recovered

This was a stunning piece of information. We knew for a fact that Celia Rose died not at Toledo but rather at the newer Lima State Hospital, to which she had been transferred in 1915. She passed away in March 1934. How could she have lived all these years in the state asyla when she was pronounced cured and released in 1897?

It seems that this is the kind of strange historical happening that will never be found in any detailed documentation. The nearest I can conjecture is based on a few bare newspaper references. On June 14, 1899, almost three years after the first poisoning, a report ran in the *Mansfield Daily Shield* headlined "Celia Rose: Report that She Is at Liberty." The article quoted a now lost issue of the *Butler Enterprise* that claimed that a rumor had ripped through Pleasant Valley that Celia Rose had been liberated from the Toledo State Hospital and was living the life of a recluse with relatives in Ross County.

"The people are much stirred up," the article said, "over the intelligence that the woman has regained her freedom."

Attorney Lewis C. Mengert, Ceely's legal guardian, was asked to comment. He said that he knew nothing of the report that Celia was at large, and if she was, it was without his knowledge or consent.

Nothing is cited as the origin of this report other than to say that it came from "a reliable source." It indicates that she was free, and the Toledo State

Hospital's admissions book supports that, stating quite plainly that she was judged cured and released. If this happened, who had taken her? With family connections already having been demonstrated in Ross County, it seems likely that she went to live with John Long or other family members who may have established contact with her once she was in the asylum.

One thing seen repeatedly in this case is the estimation by many people that Celia Rose was not insane. Removed from the situation in Pleasant Valley that had spiraled out of control, Ceely Rose settled down and apparently offered little trouble to her caregivers. Word has even passed down through family channels in the Lima area that Ceely became a favorite of the staff at that hospital.

But we know beyond a doubt that Celia Rose died in the state hospital system. So, what happened? There is no emendation or readmission entry for her in the Toledo State Hospital system. The next reference to her is in 1915, when she was transferred to the new Lima State Hospital. But a follow-up in the *Daily Shield* was published on July 24, 1899, where Sheriff Boals confirmed having seen Ceely at the Toledo State Hospital on the previous Saturday. Considering that the Toledo State Hospital was reachable by telegraph, there is no conceivable reason why it should have taken Mansfield authorities five weeks to confirm Ceely's location if she were still, in fact, a patient at the asylum.

Jerry Pearson and I conferred over this, and after reconstructing possible scenarios—none of which is provable—we came to this conclusion as to the most likely course of events: Celia Rose, not showing any evidence of being a dangerously insane patient while she was in the Toledo State Hospital, was pronounced cured and released to the only people who had made contact with her: her family from southern Ohio. It was forgotten (or, possibly, conveniently overlooked) that she was actually a ward of the state, and she was allowed to go home with her relatives in November 1897. After a year and a half, word finally made its way back to Pleasant Valley that Ceely Rose was free. It created a panic, particularly among the children of the valley, who had already started to see Ceely Rose as a sort of bogeyman figure. Attorney Mengert telegraphed the state hospital and found at that Celia had indeed been released.

Prosecuting attorney Augustus Douglass had lost his reelection bid for that position. It was largely seen as being because of the unwinnable Ceely Rose case that Douglass became unpopular. Since he had no choice but to try the case as murder in the first degree, Douglass—who was known to be a very smart character—no doubt saw the fiasco forming. He knew there was a high likelihood of losing the case. There was only one thing Douglass could do to manage the mess: he only put Celia Rose on trial for the death of her father only. When the jury found the defendant not guilty by reason of insanity, Douglass refused to nolle the remaining charges against her, and there is no statute of limitations on murder cases.

What this meant was that if Ceely were ever released from the asylum, she could be put on trial for the death of her mother and end up right back in. After that would be a trial for the murder of Walter Rose. If this game continued, there could even have been trials for the attempted murder of Mr. and Mrs. Berry and Pastor Kramer. Douglass had done the only thing he could to ensure that the murderer Ceely Rose would never again walk the streets: he gamed the system to never stop prosecuting her.

What we think must have happened was that the officials from Mansfield, including Sheriff Boals and attorney Mengert, took a little trip to southern Ohio, found Celia Rose and informed the Rose family that they had a choice: return the young woman to the Toledo State Hospital and we pretend none of this ever happened…or we arrest her and put her on trial for the death of her mother. Suddenly, without being readmitted, Ceely is once again at the Toledo State Hospital as a patient. Sheriff Boals could honestly say that he "saw" her there, omitting the detail that he was also the one who brought her back. A report sent to the Richland County auditor on December 14, 1900, listed Celia Rose as one of the forty patients from Richland County housed at the Toledo State Hospital. She never left the state asylum system again.

In 1909, state officials decided that a new, larger hospital was needed in western Ohio to deal with the volume of patients being sent into the system. A massive new building was planned—a single, massive building with multiple wings—and construction began in Lima. The largest poured-concrete building in the world at the time (a title it held until the Pentagon was built, according to local lore), the Lima State Hospital's construction was not completed until November 1914. It contained 6 million facing bricks, 2,000 windows, 50,000 panes of glass, 35 acres of plaster and 122,890 feet of electrical wire, and the distance around the building was over 1½ miles. In early 1915, patients were finally brought into the new facility, and Celia Rose was one of them.

The famous Wapakoneta, Ohio storyteller Jim Bowsher has collected stories about Ceely's status as a staff favorite at Lima. One such story—naturally unverifiable by any paperwork anywhere—is that the staff was so fond of Ceely that they decided to do something special for her in the late

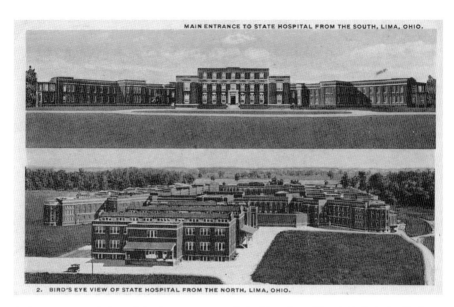

A vintage postcard view of the front entrance of the Lima State Hospital. *Author's collection.*

A vintage postcard aerial view of the Lima State Hospital shows its enormous size. *Author's collection.*

Writer, storyteller, historian and folk artist Jim Bowsher at the Temple of Tolerance in Wapakoneta, Ohio. *Author's collection.*

1920s when her health declined. The story says that the staff commandeered one of the Lima State Hospital's vehicles, and a handful of staffers loaded up Ceely and took her on a road trip.

Where was it that Ceely Rose wanted to go, the place that she chattered about incessantly? Her parents' graves. The group allegedly brought Celia to the Pleasant Valley Cemetery and helped her kneel at her family's graves and pray—something she did every single night at the hospital before going to bed.

Bowsher has collected something else, and it's a stunner. In 2003, coincidentally around the same time that I was preparing the first production of my historical drama *Ceely*, Jim was giving a speech in the Lima area. He was approached by a man after the talk who said that he had heard Jim speak before and was aware of his massive collection of stories and their related objects. He said that there was an object that his family was in possession of that he thought Jim might want.

"What's that?" Jim said.

"Ceely Rose's locket," the man said. One of the previous talks this man had heard was one where Bowsher talked about Ceely's case, which remains famous folklore in the Lima area. It was a story he didn't tell often, as he didn't have a related artifact, but this man had coincidentally caught a rare telling of it. The man explained to Jim that his family wanted to be rid of the locket because they were very unsettled by having an object in their house that belonged to a confessed murderer. But he said that if he gave Jim the locket and the backstory of how they came to have the locket, their family name was to be kept out of it. Jim took the man's name but only agreed to share this story with me on condition of anonymity for the family.

The anonymous man's father had been a guard at the Lima State Hospital. It was through this family's recollection of their father's stories that the scant information about Ceely's life in the asylum is known. The staff never had any problems with Ceely and didn't truly think she was insane. But they were aware of the legal loophole that kept her institutionalized and would for the rest of her life. She became the staff favorite and was given privileges that most patients were not. One of those was the locket. For her early months in the hospital, she asked frequently about the locket, which was her most prized possession. She said that it had been given to her by her mother, and it was the only thing of her mother's that she had left. At some point—whether in Toledo or Lima is unknown—the staff trusted Celia enough to return the locket to her, which she wore on a leather string around her neck.

That's really something to think about. A mental patient could theoretically be·very dangerous with a leather string, either to herself or to others. But they never had the slightest trouble with Ceely and the locket. What she wanted it for was to hold when she knelt down and prayed on the concrete floor beside her bed just before bedtime. She prayed for the memory and love of her parents—the very people she killed. Even when Ceely was old and infirm and the kneeling was painful, she continued the nightly ritual, clutching the locket so fervently that eventually she caved in the covers with her grip.

Celia Rose died at 8:05 p.m. on March 14, 1934, one day after her sixty-first birthday. Her death certificate was signed by Dr. A. Pfeiffer, who had been treating her since October 1930. He incorrectly rendered her first name as "Cecelia," which had never been her proper name, but it became bobbled that way in later records. Cause of death was listed as bronchopneumonia. Although it was noted that she lived at the Lima State Hospital, her profession was listed as "housework." She was buried at the cemetery for unclaimed patient bodies on Bible Road, just south of the facility. Her cross, complete with misspelled name, rests under a large tree near the back of the cemetery, which itself sits between the railroad tracks and an Ohio Department of Transportation hub.

The locket that Ceely so prized was not buried with her. It was kept as a memento of one of the staff's favorite patients and placed on display in a case near the front desk. The anonymous man who spoke to Jim Bowsher said that his father was one of the guards who worked at the hospital and knew Celia. In the 1950s, a wave of reform swept into the state hospital system. With new administrators came new practices. A hospital official saw the case with mementos of former patients and said that it was very unprofessional. According to the anonymous man, the administrator simply said that by the following day, the memento display case was to be gone. He didn't care where those things went—they just had to be removed from public display. The anonymous man's father, the guard who remembered Celia Rose fondly, grabbed the locket and took it home to prevent it from being thrown out.

For many years, the guard kept the locket. Out of respect and superstition, he didn't open it. The locket was said to have contained pictures of Ceely's parents, but between the way Ceely had dented in the covers and the corrosion that had built up around the edges of the locket, it was no longer

The cemetery for unclaimed patient bodies from the Lima State Hospital, Lima, Ohio. *Author's collection.*

Celia Rose's grave—with misspelled name—as seen in 2003, the same year Mark Sebastian Jordan premiered his historical drama *Ceely* at Malabar Farm. *Author's collection.*

Ceely's grave in 2020. A new marker has been placed since 2003, but it has deteriorated as well. Also note that a copy of the photograph of Ceely has been attached to the marker. *Author's collection.*

openable. Eventually, the guard retired and some years later passed away. The family were now left with a personal belonging of a murderer with whom they did not have a personal connection. They frankly wanted it gone from their home.

Jim Bowsher took the locket, and shortly after he received it, he hunted me down in hopes of confirming the images of the parents—if they were in there—when the locket was cleaned and opened. I told him that I had only a drawing of David Rose from the Civil War, so it wouldn't be ironclad, but that we'd at least be able to see the resemblance. Jim's brother Walt Bowsher began the process of patiently cleaning years of corrosion off the locket, and in 2004, for the first time in at least sixty-eight years (and probably longer), the locket was opened.

Inside the small locket were two mint-condition tintype photographs of David and Rebecca. It appears to be their engagement locket from 1855. The pictures were in remarkable condition, preserved no doubt by the sealed state of the locket for so many years. If the locket were held sideways, you could see how Ceely had crushed in the cover with her thumb as she

The locket that Ceely dented by clutching it fervently as she prayed for her parents. It was David and Rebecca Rose's engagement or wedding locket. *James R. Bowsher Collection.*

fervently prayed for her parents. The man in the tintype was a believable match for the later drawing of David Rose. After so much research, it was breathtaking to finally look Ceely's parents in the eyes: David's, guarded, perhaps a little lost, and Rebecca's, bold and defiant. Traits that were to run wild in Celia.

THE LEGEND RIPPLES OUTWARD

Although the news cycle of the 1890s dropped Celia Rose's story soon enough, it persisted in Pleasant Valley lore. Celia Rose gradually became a star of the campfire stories used to entertain and frighten little children. It became one of the major old legends of the place, along with Captain Pipe and Johnny Appleseed. It may have stayed there if it weren't for Louis Bromfield. The Pulitzer Prize–winning author had been a prominent literary force in the 1920s, the forgotten member of America's "Lost Generation" of writers working and drinking in France. He shifted away from high literature and more toward writing bestsellers when he saw the potential of his books being turned into Hollywood films. His novel *The Rains Came* became one of the big hits of 1938, winning the Oscar for its special effects depicting a dam burst in India.

As war's storm clouds brewed in Europe in the late 1930s, Bromfield left his friends (such as the writer Gertrude Stein) behind and brought his family home. After initially hoping to create an East Coast country estate like his friend Edith Wharton, Bromfield returned to Ohio in search of the farm of his dreams.

One day, he, his wife and his business manager had driven down to Richland County, where the author was born and raised. Driving up Pleasant Valley Road, he spied a farmhouse across the valley with a breathtaking view. He remembered seeing it in his childhood when he accompanied his father on his numerous trips all over the city and countryside. It was on one

The Clem Herring farm in 1938, the year Louis Bromfield purchased it. The barn was built with beams from the old Schrack Mill. *Ohio Department of Natural Resources/Malabar Farm State Park.*

The Berry family replaced the original house on their property with this Montgomery Ward catalogue house, which held the Malabar Farm Hostel from 1980 to 2017. *Author's collection.*

Louis Bromfield expanded Clem Herring's farmhouse into the Big House mansion, which can be toured today at Malabar Farm State Park. *Author's collection.*

of those other trips when they visited Mansfield eccentric Phoebe Wise, who was as often as not found in animated conversation with her friend, the cranky lawyer Gus Douglass. Wise was the first one to proclaim that there was something different about little Louie, something "tetched," that would mark him out for a distinctive life. Bromfield decided on the spot when he saw the beautiful valley farmhouse that it was to be his.

Bromfield piloted the car left up Hastings Road (today renamed Bromfield Road), past a Montgomery Ward catalogue house that he didn't like, across a bridge and around a curve where a small, empty cottage stood. Over the hill, he pulled into the driveway leading up to the tidy house with double front doors. Large stones had been used to shape a terrace garden at one end and formed a wall across the front yard. Bromfield got out of the car, dashed up the walkway to the front door and knocked.

Clem Herring opened the front door, and Bromfield made him an offer he couldn't refuse.

LOUIS BROMFIELD EXPANDED HERRING'S farmhouse to become his famous Big House mansion, a sprawling but comfortable thirty-two-room place that housed family, staff, friends and a constant parade of visitors ranging from neighborhood farmers up through Indian and European royalty. The place took its name, Malabar Farm, from the Malabar coast of India, which had inspired *The Rains Came.* Movie stars were often seen on the grounds, escaping Hollywood for a few days. Humphrey Bogart and Lauren Bacall were married there in 1945.

One of Bromfield's main goals with Malabar Farm was to educate the public about farming. Bromfield had once wanted to become a farmer himself but had gotten overwhelmed by trying to take over his grandfather's farm when he was a college boy with a whole semester's training in agriculture under his belt. He fled to Europe, where he served as an ambulance driver during World War I, forcing the family to sell off the ancestral farm. That haunted Bromfield, and when he saw from his high-life perch in France the destruction of farmland during the Dust Bowl, he was devastated. He decided that he wanted to do something to educate people on better farming techniques. Thus, Malabar became part experimental farm, part public showcase and part hobby farm. Bromfield began broadcasting weekly talks about farming from his office that were carried nationwide and resulted in thousands of people visiting the place.

Seeing this interest in the farm, Bromfield began writing books that directly chronicled what he was doing with farming in general and with Malabar in particular. In 1945, he published a memoir called *Pleasant Valley.* It gathered stories of Bromfield's childhood, his discovery of the Pleasant Valley property, local folklore, his ecstatic rhapsodizing about nature and his plans for revitalizing the fields of the hundreds of acres of property he had bought up, which included the homesteads originally housing the Herrings, the Roses, the Berrys and the Schracks.

In the fourth chapter of *Pleasant Valley,* Bromfield tells the story of Ceely Rose as he heard it in the valley from an old resident of a nearby town who stopped in to inquire after Bromfield's father. After hearing the story, he remembered it from his own childhood, for Bromfield himself was born in 1896, the year all the drama was taking place. Bromfield regularly changed the names of living people for their privacy, since he knew his books would be distributed worldwide. Therefore, the fact that he credits the story to a "Mr. Charles," likely means nothing. Indeed, although Bromfield uses the names of the Rose family members, he changed Guy Berry's name to

Pulitzer Prize–winning author and conservationist Louis Bromfield with his daughters Ellen (*center*) and Hope, as well as some of their boxers. The terrace garden behind them was built with foundation stones from the Schrack Mill. *Ohio Department of Natural Resources/Malabar Farm State Park.*

After the Rose family's deaths, Clem Herring brought the old Schrack Mill, seen here in about 1897, just before it was torn down. He used stones and beams from the mill all over his farm. *Ohio Department of Natural Resources/Malabar Farm State Park.*

Hugh Fleming because Guy was still alive at the time and probably not a bit happy that the story was being dug up again.

It's a mangled version of the story in *Pleasant Valley*, for Bromfield obviously didn't check for accuracy by cross-referencing any of the details he was given. In this version, the Rose family was originally from Tennessee, an obvious exaggeration of their Appalachian roots. Hugh Fleming is portrayed as older than Ceely, which Guy Berry was in mental age, at least. Here, Hugh Fleming tells Ceely that he would like to be with her, but their parents don't approve. Ceely soaks the arsenic out of flypaper and mixes it in with the cottage cheese she serves at breakfast, but in this telling the family is parents and two brothers, perhaps a misremembered version of the fact that there was, once, an additional sibling. Tracy Davis becomes in Bromfield's narrative Vilma Smith, also from Tennessee. Vilma fills Ceely with a big meal, and then they go into the barn to lie in the sweet-smelling hay, talking drowsily. The sheriff and prosecuting attorney suddenly step out and arrest Ceely after her confession. The mill wheel turned no more, and the miller's house was empty until the neighbor bought the property, rented out the house, tore down the massive mill and built a new cattle barn out of it.

Above: The Big Barn at Malabar Farm is a reconstruction of the original barn, which stood here but burned in a fire in 1993. The new barn was raised in 1996. *Author's collection*.

Opposite: The northeast corner of the barn utilized some of the original beams from the Schrack Mill that survived the burning of the barn in 1993. *Author's collection*.

In Bromfield's telling, that neighbor is named Clem Anson, which is of course Clem Herring. Herring indeed bought the mill and built his barn out of it. That became Malabar Farm's main barn, which stood until 1993, when it burned down. A few of the historic beams that had not been scorched were saved and used in 1996, when the Timber Frame Guild of America held a barn raising at Malabar, rebuilding the barn and including the salvaged pieces of the old Schrack Mill, which can today be found in the northeast corner of the upper level of the barn.

Bromfield didn't fact-check the folkloric version of the story that came to him, but he caught its essence powerfully. When *Pleasant Valley* became one of his best-selling books, it was translated and distributed worldwide. Later memoirs like 1948's *Malabar Farm* kept the momentum going, making Bromfield's project the most famous farm in America. Ceely's story circulated internationally.

As I noted in the introduction, I first encountered the story of Ceely Rose in an Associated Press article that was first circulated in 1978 and again, when I saw it, in 1982. I heard the story directly while visiting Malabar

Farm, which had become a state park in the 1970s, after being run by the nonprofit organization The Friends of the Land after Bromfield's death in 1956, until 1972. The farm's wagon tours stopped to tell the story of Ceely Rose, although they always used Bromfield's version of the story, complete with altered names.

In 1994, I read Chris Woodyard's *Haunted Ohio*, which consulted original news clippings to reconstruct the story without Bromfield's inaccuracies. I was inspired to attempt a dramatization of the story after undertaking extensive research. I wrote my first draft of *Ceely* in 1995 in one week. I tried to write the piece in a style that would reflect the time when the story took place, using the deterministic, stark style of the realism that had entered literature in the late 1800s in the works of such writers as Stephen Crane and Frank Norris. I showed a draft of it to the professor of theater at the Ohio State University's Mansfield campus, Dr. Larry Evans. He blasted the work, saying that it was "cold and melodramatic" and that not only would he never direct it, but if it were produced, he also wouldn't even go see it.

That put it on ice for some time. I was prepared to leave the script in a drawer to collect dust, but as I began doing more theater, including directing, my frequent collaborator Daniel J. Feiertag, who often served as my technical director, refused to let me neglect the play, which he had read. He convinced me to dust it off and give it another look. He even went so far as to scan in my original typewritten script so that I could revise it on a computer, as I had recently bought a used Macintosh to write on. I revised the script but made no particular attempt to tone down its starkness. I sent the play off to a competition being held by the Ohio Theatre Alliance, where it was awarded an honorable mention. Because of a rehearsal for a production of one-act plays I was involved with at OSU–Mansfield, I would not be able to attend the OTA conference to collect my award. Dr. Evans overheard my remark and said that he'd be going to the conference and would be glad to pick up the certificate for me. I didn't tell him that the award was for *Ceely*. He discovered that when he accepted the award on my behalf.

With a workable script now in hand, I approached a local community theater, the Mansfield Playhouse, and tried to interest it in my script. The second-oldest continually producing community theater in the state of Ohio, the Playhouse was restricted by overhead costs of a vintage building, so it was leery of producing anything that wasn't already popular, let alone something unpublished and unproven. So back in the drawer it went.

Dan Feiertag kept bringing it up periodically, to my general indifference. But around 2002, he finally said, "We have to produce *Ceely*. It's too cool not to." This time, I went down to Malabar Farm State Park and inquired with park manager Louis Andres about the possibility of maybe doing the drama somewhere outside at Malabar.

"Why not just do it in the barn?" Andres said. "We already have a stage built in there." He took me out to the rebuilt barn and showed me the small stage that stood at one end of the upper level. The stage had been built to use for special events and as a bandstand when they held barn dances. I realized it was perfect.

Armed with an ideal venue—a venue that included pieces of one of the original structures central to the story—I approached the Mansfield Playhouse again, with the idea of doing a co-production with Malabar Farm via the Malabar Farm Foundation, a long-standing nonprofit organization that promotes Louis Bromfield's legacy. Louis Andres and I engineered a budget that would charge the production for use of the space, but any equipment bought for the production would afterward become property of the Playhouse. Dinner would be included, catered by Lucas-based Port-a-Cook, and profits, if any, would be divided up evenly between the Mansfield Playhouse and the Malabar Farm Foundation.

Left: Actress Candy Boyd created the lead role in *Ceely* in 2003 and reprised the role a year later. *Author's collection.*

Right: Rhiannon Evans played Ceely in 2007 and 2008. The decorative hex sign was designed and created for the productions by Mark Sebastian Jordan, Robert Hutchison and Daniel J. Feiertag. *Author's collection.*

This time, the Playhouse bit, and we were able to slate the production for the fall of 2003 with the help of a project kickoff grant from the Richland County Foundation.

In addition to Dan's goading me, I was also ready to go forward with the production because I had found a young Playhouse actress, Candy Boyd, who had the explosive intensity to play the role of Ceely Rose. Candy and I worked on the role for months before rehearsals even began, and she played the part the first two years, 2003 and 2004. When we returned to *Ceely* in 2007 and 2008, the role was played by Rhiannon Evans, who endearingly explored the shyer nuances of the character. When we revived it in 2012, the lead role was played by Jennifer Casner, who gave it a whole new level by physicalizing Ceely's obsessive mannerisms. I would be remiss if I didn't also point out that the counterweight to Ceely in the show, Rebecca, was played with great dignity and humanity by first Char

Hutchison and later by Jacqueline Allen. Numerous other actors brought the piece to life unforgettably.

As those production dates above suggest, *Ceely* was a hit. All the tickets sold out before the first performances of the first production and continued to sell out in later years. This platform allowed me to later write *Phoebe*, about Phoebe Wise (2005, 2006), and I completed *The Malabar Trilogy* with *Louie*, about Bromfield himself, in 2010 and 2011. After a partly acted, part storytelling revival of *Ceely* in 2015, we decided to let the productions end, as it had become increasingly difficult to find actors willing to travel out to Malabar and virtually impossible to schedule things in the barn, which was constantly being rented out by the state park.

Dozens of cast and crew members experienced the adventures of these productions, in a working barn open to elements that might be stifling hot one day and frigidly cold the next. The layout of the barn and the use of side stages put actors within inches of audience members. Most of all, I remember that the informality of the setting—we were in a barn, for goodness sake, with goats cackling downstairs—removed audience members' inhibitions. They would get so caught up in the drama that when a line of comic relief was introduced, the crowds would explode in laughter before we started screwing the tension even tighter. I'm proud of the run we had. In answer to the constant questions I receive about reviving the shows, I can only say that I have no idea if conditions will ever be right to do those shows again.

In the later productions of *Ceely*, we were able to make use (with permission and a paid royalty fee) of a song that had been written by the Indiana folk singer Tim Grimm in 2005. I contacted him after stumbling across his song on the Internet, on Grimm's album *The Back Fields*. Tim told me that he had written the song after visiting the house of a friend of his who lived in Ohio. They had planned to do something outdoors that day, but the weather ended up being wall-to-wall rain. Looking for something to do, Grimm started looking through his friend's books and noticed a book called *Pleasant Valley* by someone named Louis Bromfield. Grimm had never heard of the book or the author, but it looked like an intriguing blend of storytelling and rural life, so he sat down to read. When he encountered Celia Rose's story, it grabbed him, and the lines started coming. He wrote a chilling, haunting song based on Bromfield's version of the story. Although the names and details were sometimes different for this reason, it remains a potent distillation of the tale.

In 2007, historian Brett J. Mitchell put together a photo history of the case titled *Triple Murder: The Crimes Committed by Celia Rose*. It was the first detailed examination of this case, and I was glad to have worked closely with Brett on research during that period. Since the book is no longer in print, I hope that this book restores many images (plus a few new ones) from the same archival sources to widespread public availability, while going into new detail about the case.

A most amazing and unlikely artifact emerged in 2013 when historian James Dailey II found an astonishing image in a set of photographs he purchased. The collection was images from the Lima State Hospital and included shots from a publicity event held in 1917. It was apparently a sort of public exhibition to demonstrate how patients were being taught practical life skills so that they would be employable when released from the asylum. The administrators of the hospital staged a photo op, featuring a row of female patients demonstrating that they had learned how to hammer nails into wooden planks.

Toward the right end of the row is a familiar face. Is it Celia Rose? Dailey said that there is no documentation to prove that it was, but the resemblance is startling. And we know that Ceely was a special favorite of the staff there, so who would be a better choice for a photo op than a highly functioning favorite patient? If it is Ceely, it's astonishing to think they would present

Patient Vocation Day at the Lima State Hospital, circa 1917. *James Dailey II—The Dailey Archives.*

her—a confessed triple murderer—in an image brandishing a hammer. Perhaps that's the reason this photo never seems to have circulated publicly. If not for Dailey's location of it, the photo might never have surfaced. As it is, it is a strong candidate to be the second known photograph of Celia Rose. Dailey will in the future be publishing a book to reveal the other gems he has collected in the Dailey Archives.

Is this cheerful hammering mental patient Celia Rose? There is no documentation, but the startling resemblance—and Ceely's known status as a staff favorite—makes it possible. *James Dailey II—The Dailey Archives.*

Literally the day before I received the final edit of this book for review from my editor, Ryan Finn, I virtually stumbled across another astonishing connection to this case. While examining a genealogy website, I saw a link to the blog *Wandering Appalachia*, which had just published an extensively researched post about the 1921 murder of John Newman and Louise Doyle, which occurred north of Portsmouth, Ohio, along the Scioto Trail. As Newman was married to another woman, the deaths were initially examined as a jealousy killing, with murder/suicide having been ruled out by the lack of a gun at the crime scene.

Investigators found Newman's car abandoned a few miles away and began to explore the notorious figures who lived nearby. One such person was Roy Chamblin, a young man with a wooden leg due to an earlier railroad accident. He was suspected of holding up and robbing travelers, but no proof had been found with which to build a case against him. But when the Scioto County sheriff searched Chamblin's residence, he found blood-soaked clothes. A wanted bulletin was released, and police in Cincinnati found Chamblin at a relative's place. The suspect did not resist arrest and was returned to Portsmouth. He wasn't grilled for long before he admitted that he shot Newman and Doyle, but he denied that robbery was the motive. Chamblin claimed that Newman threw a brick at him and that his shots were in self-defense. No brick having been found at the crime scene, it was obvious that Chamblin's story was a ploy to avoid the electric chair.

Newspaper reports state that Chamblin showed no remorse or empathy for his victims. He only became emotional when the sheriff asked Roy what his mother would think when she heard about what he had done. That choked him up. He asked if he could speak to his uncle about how to break the news to his mother. The report then says that Chamblin's maternal uncle, Ora Easter, was called into the jail to see Chamblin.

I slammed on the brakes of my reading and stared at the uncle's surname. Easter? Easter is not a particularly common surname. Ceely Rose's mother, Rebecca, was an Easter. Rebecca was born in Highland County, which is not far away from Scioto County: at their closest point, the two counties stand less than ten miles apart. I began plunging into genealogical sources, tracing various branches of the southern Ohio Easters. Ora Easter's sister was Eva Easter. Although she remarried later, Eva's first husband was Homer Chamblin, Roy's father. Eva's father was Jacob P. Easter (1844–1917), son of John Frederick Easter (1805–1868), son of Nicholas Easter (1767–1833). Nicholas also had a son named Jacob (1801–1889), who was the father of Rebecca, Ceely Rose's mother. Roy Chamblin was Ceely Rose's second cousin, once removed.

At the end of Chamblin's trial, the jury found him guilty of double murder, and the judge sentenced him to die in the electric chair. Chamblin accepted his fate calmly, saying that his whole life he "never had a chance." Was he simply bemoaning his unlucky fate, or did he know something about the instability that had led his cousin down the road to murder just twenty-five years earlier? No one knows. The connection has never been noted before.

Roy Chamblin was executed in the State of Ohio's electric chair, infamously known as "Old Sparky," at the Ohio Penitentiary in Columbus on March 24, 1922. The chair today is housed in the Ohio Corrections Museum, which is inside the Ohio State Reformatory in Mansfield, just thirteen miles away from Malabar Farm. Considering that I have frequently worked at the reformatory as a tour guide and was on set as a background actor in 1993 when *The Shawshank Redemption* was filmed at the reformatory, it is especially astonishing to me to uncover a connection between the Ceely Rose story and the infamous penal institution. Dig deep, and the connections will be found.

My own retellings of the Ceely Rose story and its associated ghost stories have spread far and wide. I have done personal appearances and radio interviews all over Ohio, I've been interviewed on Internet programs and

I've even been involved with television productions talking about it, such as *Ghost Hunters* in 2013 and the pilot *House of the Unknown*, shot in 2007. Occasionally, I do an online search to see how far Ceely Rose's story has rippled out. It is now appearing in languages I don't even recognize.

What is it about Celia Rose's story that keeps it nagging at our collective cultural memory? Perhaps it is simply that Ceely proves there are no easy answers in real life. On one level, it's a coldblooded murder story. On another, it is a story of unrequited love. On at least one level, it is a story of a girl who loved her parents yet committed a destructive act far more devastating than she ever knew it could be. It's a story of Appalachian people being looked down on by northerners. It's a story of country folk versus city folk. It's a story of guilt and a story of innocence. It's a story about how a tiny piece of American folklore can sweep around the world. In the end, it is finally a mystery, because Celia Rose—the girl dismissed as silly, an imbecile—was all these things. And none of them.

EPILOGUE

The Dream Mill

Great-grandfather nods in his corner,
And dreams of the long ago;
He tells me the tales of his dream mill,
And of friends he used to know.

I see his old wheel in the winter—
Its fuzzy, icy chin;
The silvery hair and the whiskers,
The frozen, frosty grin.

I see him alone in his corner;
I crawl up on his knee.
We sing the old song of his dream mill,
And the days that used to be:

Turn again, old dreamland mill,
Turn your silent wheel!
Fill our waiting, wobbly sacks
Full of golden meal.

Turn us back to happy days,
Boyhood's carefree thrill—
Slowly, slowly, slowly turn,
Silent dreamland mill.

By Flora Schrack, published in 1941.

APPENDICES

The Last Will & Testament of Rebecca Rose

On the 18th day of July, 1896
Rebecca Rose of Monroe Twp, Richland County, Ohio Being in her last sickness at her home near Newville O, aforesaid co. and state. In the presence of the undersigned witnesses did declare her last will concerning her disposition of her Personal and real estate as follows.

1st I give to my daughter Celia Rose and my Grandson John H Long the bidding of the house to be divided equally between them.

2. I give to the above named Celia Rose and John H Long, the ballance [sic] of my personal Estate and all my real Estate after paying any just debts, to be sold by my administration hereafter named and the proceeds to be divided equally between them.

3. I want Clement M. Herring to be my Administrator.

At the time said Rebecca Rose stated the foregoing as her will. She was of sound mind and meaning and not under any restraint.

And she then and there called upon us to hear testimony to said disposition as he will. Reduced to writing by me on this 22nd day of July, 1896.

(signed)
Phebe Herring
Clement M. Herring
A.W. Budd

The State of Ohio
Richland County

Before me, Lewis Brucker, Judge of the Probate Court of Richland County, personally appeared Phebe Herring, Clement M. Herring, and AW Budd, who being duly sworn say that they were present on the 18th day of July 1896 at the residence of Rebecca Rose in Monroe Township, Richland County, Ohio, and did hear Rebecca Rose utter what is specified in the foregoing writing, that she was at that time of sound mind and memory, and not under any restraint and that she at the time the testamentary words were spoken called upon them to bear testimony to said disposition as her will, and that said Rebecca Rose was then in her last sickness, to the best of their knowledge and belief.

(signed)
PHEBE HERRING
AW BUDD
CLEMENT M. HERRING

Sworn to and subscribed before me this 22nd day of July A.D. 1896.

(signed)
LEWIS BRUCKER
JUDGE OF THE PROBATE COURT OF RICHLAND COUNTY OHIO

Judge Lewis Brucker oversaw the filing of Rebecca Rose's final will and testament. *Timothy Brian McKee Collection.*

A Bill of the Property sold by C.M. Herring, Exr, of the Estate of Rebecca Rose, Dec'd, late of Richland County, deceased, at Public Vendue. August 15th, A.D. 1896.

Page 1

No. of Items	Description as Inventoried	Value	To Whom Sold	Price
1	box of books	$0.25	W.H. McFarland	$0.40
-	bottles	$0.05	C.M. Colins	$0.05
1	bu. basket & cans	$0.10	Mrs. Kinton	$0.05
3	jugs & pitcher	$0.10	Mrs. S. Berry	$0.05
4	jugs	$0.10	"	$0.05
8	cans & jars	$0.10	Mrs. Herring	$0.05
5	crocks & jars	$0.10	Mrs. Davis	$0.05
6	cans & "	$0.30	Mrs. S. Andrews	$0.05
6	do [ditto]	$0.25	Mrs. Pritchard	$0.05
6	cans cherrys	$0.30	Mrs. Carlisle	$0.25
6	do	$0.30	Mrs. S. Andrews	$0.25
3	brooms & rack	$0.05	Mrs. S. Berry	$0.10
-	dish pan & board	$0.15	Mrs. S. Andrews	$0.21
3	bake pans	$0.15	-	-
1	dipper	$0.05	J. Disbro	$0.05
1	water bucket	$0.15	Mrs. Colins	$0.10
2	bells	$0.05	-	-
1	bucket & eggs	$0.05	Mrs. Andrews	$0.10
-	water pitcher	$0.20	Alice Mitchell	$0.40
-	" "	$0.05	Geo. Anderson	$0.30

-	bowl & eggs	$0.10	" "	$0.35
2	razors & strop	$0.15	C Mutersbaugh	$0.40
1	pr. nippers	$0.10	S. Andrews	$0.10
-	ammunition box	$0.05	C. Charles	$0.05
1	hatchet	$0.10	Geo. Anderson	$0.10
-	basket, pan & bucket	$0.05	Mary Pitts	$0.05
1	sieve	$0.05	-	-
3	bake pans	$0.05	Mrs. S. Berry	$0.10
1	mirror	$0.05	Miss Swigart	$0.05
3	pans	$0.05	G.A. Davis	$0.15

Page 2

No. of Items	Description as Inventoried	Value	To Whom Sold	Price
2	frying pans	$0.10	Geo Anderson	$0.20
-	coffee pot & pan	$0.05	John Disbro	$0.10
-	pot lids & qt. meas.	$0.05	S. Berry	$0.05
2	skimmers	$0.05	Mrs. Pritchard	$0.10
2	tin buckets	$0.10	Mrs. S. Berry	$0.10
6	" cups	$0.05	John Ohler	$0.13
1	steamer	$0.15	" "	$0.20
6	8 in pans & 2 ladles	$0.10	Mrs. C. Colins	$0.10
1	jar & dish pan	$0.10	Allie Berry	$0.10
1	brass kettle	$0.30	J.W. Baughman	$0.80
1	spring scale	$0.10	Earn Baughman	$0.05
1	roast pan	$0.05	John Ohler	$0.15
1	water bucket b.h.	$0.10	" "	$0.15

1	dash lantern	$0.15	Chas. Mutersbaugh	$0.40
1	" "	$0.05	Mrs. Herring	$0.20
1	" "	$0.05	L. Berry	$0.20
1	" "	$0.05	J. Jones	$0.17
2	goblets & g. dish	$0.05	broke	-
10	plates & dish	$0.10	Mrs. Andrews	$0.36
2	pitchers	$0.10	John Ohler	$0.15
1	coffee mill	$0.20	Susan Berry	$0.30
1	set 6 knives	$0.15	Geo. Anderson	$0.30
1	coffee jar	$0.05	-	-
1	tea can	$0.05	Mrs. Whittimire	$0.10
-	½ bushel measure	$0.05	-	-
4	tin cans	$0.05	G.A. Davis	$0.08
-	cups & saucers	$0.05	" "	$0.13
-	plate & bowls	$0.05	Mrs. H. Charles	$0.10
1	sugar b & 6 pitchers	$0.10	Mrs. Pitts	$0.05
1	soap dish	$0.05	Allie Snider	$0.10
-	1½ lbs coffee	$0.15	John Waugerman	$0.20
1	large lamp	$0.10	Mrs. Tarris	$0.23
1	lamp	$0.05	P. Baughman	$0.10
1	candle m. & propper	$0.05	J. Waugerman	$0.05
1	candle & s. chain	$0.05	Mrs Colins	$0.05
1	strainer bucket	$0.15	Mr. McDanel [sic]	$0.05
-	butterbowl &tc.	$0.20	J. Cole	$0.30

Page 3

No. of Items	Description as Inventoried	Value	To Whom Sold	Price
1	sack carpet rags	$0.05	J. Ohler	$0.05
1	[ditto]	$0.05	G.A. Davis	$0.05
1	box	$0.05	Geo Anderson	$0.14
1	feather bed	$0.25	Mrs. Paulins	$0.76
2	boxes	$0.05	Miss Swigart	$0.10
1	table	$0.25	John Ohler	$0.85
1	stand	$0.10	Mrs. McDermott	$0.55
1	rocker	$0.05	-	-
1	rustic chair	$0.25	Mrs. Swigart	$0.85
6	brown chairs	$1.00	John Ohler	$2.50
1	duster	$0.25	Ezra Snyder	$0.80
1	robe	$1.00	Newton Hersh	$1.55
1	lot scrap cask	$0.25	McDermott	$0.25
1	lot scrap cask	$0.50	Geo. Anderson	$0.20
1	" " "	$0.40	J. Waugerman	$1.70
1	roll carpet	$0.50	J. Waugerman	$2.60
1	parlor stove	$2.00	Mrs. Berry	$8.00
1	sewing machine	$10.00	J. Charles	$19.50
1	mirror	$0.25	Ezra Snyder	$0.55
1	clock	$1.00	C. Mutersbaugh	$1.70
1	bedstead	$0.50	Mrs. Colins	$1.50
1	bureau	$0.50	John Hunter	$0.80
1	clock	$0.05	-	-
1	box sap spiles	$1.00	[illegible] Snider	$0.30

1	stocking yarn	$0.25	" "	$0.20
2	parasols	$0.05	-	-
1	sack beans	$0.05	Geo. Anderson	$0.15
5 lbs	carpet chain	$0.50	G.A. Davis	$0.45

Page 4

No. of Items	Description as Inventoried	Value	To Whom Sold	Price
5	bars lead	$0.10	G.W. Berry	$0.10
10	lbs 8/un. nails	$0.15	A Berry	$0.25
6	box sealing wax	$0.15	[ditto?]	$0.05
6	" matches	$0.90	D. Hunter	$0.70
2	spigots	$0.10	Snider	$0.25
5	papers coffee es	$0.10	Hunter	$0.05
2	" coffee	$0.20	Snavely	$0.32
1	box raisins	[ditto?]	P. Baughman	$0.25
1	meat barrel	$1.25	J. Hunter	$1.20
2	iron rods	$0.10	M. Snyder	$0.05
1	screen door	$0.10	[missed]	-
1	ham 19 lbs 4¢	$0.75	G.A. Davis	$1.00
1	" "	$0.75	" "	$1.10
1	" 17½	$0.70	F. Taylor	$1.15
1	" 18½	$0.75	J. Marks	$1.10
1	" 17	$0.70	F. Taylor	$1.15
1	side 11 lbs 3¢	$0.30	G. Davis	$0.85
1	" 10	$0.30	D. Hunter	$0.85
1	bunch paper sacks	$0.05	Geo. Yates	$0.20

| 1 | roll tarred paper | $0.10 | - | - |
| 1 | pile shingles | $0.40 | P. Baughman | $0.15 |

Page 5

No. of Items	Description as Inventoried	Value	To Whom Sold	Price
-	match box etc	$0.15	Mrs. Ohler	$0.30
1	box locks	$0.20	P. Baughman	$0.32
3	smoothing irons	$0.15	J. Waugerman	$0.20
1	pot	$0.20	G.A. Davis	$0.65
1	stove shelf	$0.15	W.A. Wallace	$0.25
-	shovel h. & ax	$0.05	S. Berry	$0.10
1	cookstove & pipe	$2.00	S.A. Tucker	$4.50
1	skillet	$0.15	Mrs. Pealer	$0.15
1	large skillet	$0.15	S.K. Charles	$0.30
1	dinner pot	$0.15	J.H. Rummer	$0.20
1	flat d. pot	$0.15	S. Andrews	$0.15
1	tea kettle	$0.15	Mrs. McDaniel	$0.05
1	gasoline stove	$2.00	C. Mutersbaugh	$8.25
1	safe	$0.50	Mrs. Ohler	$1.00
1	double cupboard	$0.50	Mrs. Pealer	$1.15
1	table	$0.60	C. Robinson	$0.50
1	old chairs	$0.20	Mrs. McDermott	$0.50
1	(illegible) flour	$0.50	P. Baughman	$0.50
1	sieve & dipper	$0.10	Allie Berry	$0.10
1	cellar cupboard	$0.10	W.A. Wallace	$0.40
1	vinegar b & cont.	$1.00	-	-

2	paint buckets	$0.05	-	-
1	towel & roller	$0.05	-	-
-	box & 4 chimneys	$0.10	P. Baughman	$0.10
8	box r h menders	$0.10	"	$0.44
8	window glass	$0.25	L.L. Snider	$0.25
1	wash stand	$0.25	John Ohler	$0.50
1	sack carpet	$0.05	Mrs. Carlisle	$0.25

Page 6

No. of Items	Description as Inventoried	Value	To Whom Sold	Price
2	planes	$0.10	-	-
2	bolts & mallet	$0.05	C.E. Norris	$0.05
1	side saddle	$0.50	Newton Hersh	$2.40
1	square sap pan	$0.25	Smith	$0.90
1	[illegible]	-	-	-
2	saws	$0.10	Geo. Anderson	$0.10
1	saw	$0.50	F. Berry	$0.52
1	Eureka F[anning] mill	$8.00	C.F. Gladden	$9.00
10	bu[shel] corn & oats 44 lb	$1.50	-	-
25	" corn 20¢	$5.00	Geo. Anderson 10 bu	$2.20
-	-	-	Frank Taylor 21 bu	$5.00
50	bu corn & oats 44 lb 15¢	$7.50	Geo Yates 10 bu 15¢	$1.50
-	W.A. Wallace 15 bu 14¢	$2.10	W.A. Wallace 15 bu 14¢	$2.10
-	-	-	" 10 bu 15¢	$1.50

-	-	-	" 10 bu 15¢	$1.50
1	lb brand	$0.30	H.N. Ruth	$0.55
5	bu wheat 45¢	$2.25	6 bu W.A. Wallace 50¢	$3.00
12	bu wheat 45¢	$5.40	-	-
1	grain cradle	$1.00	J.C. Tucker	$1.40
1	oil can	$0.25	H.N. Ruth	$0.05
1	sack truck	$0.75	J.M. Darling	$2.15
1	lb crackers	$0.10	J. Ohler	$0.25
33	lb sugar	$1.00	J. Jones	$1.56
1	lard press	$1.00	G.W. Berry	$3.10
1	meat chopper	$1.00	" "	$1.10
½	keg of spikes	$0.50	D. Hunter	$0.85

Page 7

No. of Items	Description as Inventoried	Value	To Whom Sold	Price
1	4 tined fork & shovel	$0.05	-	-
1	poke & bridle	$0.05	-	-
1	fly net	$0.25	Pritchard	$0.40
1	set single harness	$2.00	Geor. Anderson	$3.10
-	straps & harness	$1.00	C. Gretzinger	$0.55
-	comb & brush	$0.05	P. Heck	$0.10
1	lb. & chop	$0.05	J. Hunter	$0.05
-	hame, snap & bolt	$0.05	S. McKonkie	$0.26
-	[missed]	-	-	-
1	oil barrel	$0.10	Wm. Swigart	$0.10
1	"	$0.15	G.W. Berry	$0.15

-	spreader chain etc	$0.05	J. Hunter	$0.10
-	iron of wagon	$0.25	H.N. Ruth	$0.05
-	harness	$0.15	Wm. Swigart	$0.25
-	double tree, neck yokes	$0.05	E.E. Huston	$0.10
-	buggy pole & fills	$0.05	H.N. Ruth	$0.10
-	strap iron & handles	$0.10	-	-
-	2 rakes	$0.10	M. Snyder	$0.15
1	shovel	$0.20	Anderson	$0.55
2	axes	$0.10	J.B. Wiles	$0.40
1	mattock	$0.25	W.E. Jones	$0.40
1	I. pick	$0.30	Geo. Anderson	$0.55
1	mowing scythe	$0.25	J.M. Darling	$0.20
1	1m auger	$0.10	N.E. Smiths	$0.15
1	m. wrench	$0.10	H. Rummel	$0.20
1	pair pinchers	$0.10	J.T. Rowe	$0.10
1	lock chain	$0.05	Pritchard	$0.15

Page 8

No. of Items	Description as Inventoried	Value	To Whom Sold	Price
2	box sealing wax	$0.05	Geor. McKonkie	$0.05
6	papers coffee extract	$0.05	S. McFarlane	$0.20 total
4	box baking powder	$0.10	"	-
1	lb starch	$0.05	"	-
4	papers alspice & gin[ger]	$0.10	Geo. Anderson	$0.40 total

3	papers pins	$0.05	"	-
2	alspice & cloves	$0.05	"	-
1	lb black tea	$0.10	"	-
1	qr "	$0.05	"	-
1	paper nutmeg	$0.05	"	-
1	cake soap & pepper	$0.05	Pealer	$0.30 total
13	lead pencils	$0.40	"	-
11	carpenter pencils	$0.25	"	$0.20
2	lbs raisins	$0.05	John Disbro	$0.20 total
2	lbs prunes	$0.05	"	-
2	lbs raisins	$0.05	P. Baughman	$0.05
2	lbs r oats	$0.05	Geo. Anderson	$0.15
1	lb sulphur	$0.05	J. Disbro	$0.25 total
2	lbs rice	$0.05	-	-
2	papers sugar	$0.05	-	-
4	papers tea	$0.05	-	-
60	chickens	$5.00	J. Moffat	$1.53
-	-	-	Frank Shanabarger	$1.70
-	-	-	W.E. Jones	$2.70
-	-	-	Ira Beverage	$5.88
1	saddle	$0.10	Joe Hosepelt	$0.80
-	buggy lines	$0.20	Jeff Frontz	$0.60
1	fork	$0.10	T.B. Wiles	$0.25

Page 9

No. of Items	Description as Inventoried	Value	To Whom Sold	Price
1	4 gal[lon] jar	$0.05	J. Tucker	$0.10
1	8 gal jar	$0.05	G.A. Davis	$0.15
1	20 gal gasoline can	$0.30	H.N. Ruth	$0.60
2	tubs	$0.10	J. Hunter	$0.20
1	steel trap	$0.05	McCreedy	$0.05
2	1 gal crocks	$0.05	G.A. Davis	$0.10
"	" "	$0.05	G.W. Berry	$0.12
2	" "	$0.05	" "	$0.06
2	2 gal crocks	$0.10	G.A. Davis	$0.15
2	" "	$0.10	" "	$0.15
2	" "	$0.10	" "	$0.15
2	" "	$0.10	Mrs. Charles	$0.26
1	kettle	$0.05	F.J. Taylor	$0.05
1	kettle with legs	$0.80	A. Berry	$2.30
1	r bottom kettle	$0.50	F.J. Taylor	$2.00
½	lb ½ full soap	$0.25	G.A. Davis	$0.35
1	old churn	$0.05	-	-
1	single cord wood	$0.50	H.N. Ruth	$0.10
8	"	$2.00	"	41¢ ($3.28)
1	box thread	$0.30	"	$0.25
1	" "	$0.20	"	$0.25
	½ box	$0.15	J. Schrack	$0.21
1	"	$0.15	Geo. Yates	$0.10
1	"	$0.25	J. Schrack	$0.33
3	papers tobacco	$0.10	F. Baughman	$0.07

1	box matches	$0.15	Geo. Anderson	$0.18
1	small box matches	$0.05	C.A. Flemming	$0.05
4	lbs soda	$0.10	John Ohler	$0.10

Page 10

No. of Items	Description as Inventoried	Value	To Whom Sold	Price
-	boiler & bucket	$0.05	-	-
-	stove pipe	$0.05	-	-
-	oil cloth	$0.25	Wm. Swigart	$0.15
1	stove zinc	$0.05	H.N. Ruth	$0.10
-	ax & rope	$0.10	Geo. Anderson	$0.10
-	washing machine	$0.50	S. Andrews	$2.60
5	gal oil can	$0.25	Wm. Pealer	$0.05
4	" pump can	$0.10	J. Marks	$0.10
-	scrap carpet	$0.05	Julia Pealer	$0.05
-	ax & wedge	$0.20	T.B. Wiles	$0.20
-	keg & vinegar	$0.50	Geo. Anderson	$0.35
-	stone drill & bolt	$0.05	C. Robinson	$0.05
-	buck saw	$0.15	H.L. Charles	$0.15
-	hand saw	$0.05	P. Baughman	$0.10
1	cow chain	$0.05	Mrs. Rowe	$0.05
1	1 man saw	$0.25	Geo. Anderson	$0.80
3	1 gal cans	$0.15	-	-
1	keg spikes etc	$0.10	John Hunter	$0.05
1	stove	[missed]	J.C. Tucker	$3.00
-	thermometer	$0.10	W.A. Wallace	$0.29
-	churn & strainer	$0.10	John Tarris	$0.30
2	jars	$0.10	Mrs. S. Berry	$0.10

160

2	jugs & jars	$0.05	-	-
5	jars & 1 jug	$0.05	S.A. Tucker	$0.10
4	jars	$0.10	Mrs. Limes	$0.10
1	crock & lard	$0.10	-	-
1	crock & tallow	$0.10	John Disbro	$0.05
1	8 gal jar & can	$0.10	M. Snyder	$0.10

Page 11

No. of Items	Description as Inventoried	Value	To Whom Sold	Price
1	can lard	$2.00	G.A. Davis	$4.10
1	" "	$2.00	Joe Jones	$2.80
1	" "	$2.00	S. Colins	$2.75
1	carpet loom	$1.50	Mrs. H.L. Charles	$3.75
-	chairs paint etc	$0.05	G.A. Davis	$0.10
1	½ gal jug syrup	$0.10	E.A. Barry	$0.15
1	" " " "	$0.10	" "	$0.15
1	" " " "	$0.10	" "	$0.15
1	gal syrup	$0.25	" "	$0.45
1	" "	$0.25	" "	$0.45
1	" "	$0.25	" "	$0.45
1	" "	$0.25	W.A. Wallace	$0.45
1	" "	$0.25	" "	$0.45
1	" "	$0.25	P. Baughman	$0.45
1	crock & butter	$0.20	J Wangerman	$0.10
1	gal grapes	$0.20	J.T. Rowe	$0.05
1	jar corn	$0.05	C.E. Norris	$0.10

1	"	$0.05	J.T. Rowe	$0.05
1	"	$0.05	-	-
-	stove pipe	$0.10	S. Colins	$0.05
1	grubbing hoe	$0.05	M.H. Schrack	$0.15
2	buckets	$0.05	-	-
-	sprinkling can	$0.05	W. Pealer	$0.25
2	buckets	$0.10	J. Frontz	$0.10
-	garden hoe & rake	$0.15	Reverend Kramer	$0.15
-	x cut saw	$0.25	J. Wallace	$0.25
1	wringer	$0.50	G.W. Berry	$1.00
1	washboard	$0.10	James Secrist	$0.50

Page 12

No. of Items	Description as Inventoried	Value	To Whom Sold	Price
1	oil barrel	$0.15	Geo. Anderson	$0.30
-	oil measure & funnel	$0.10	-	-
-	wheelbarrow	$0.25	C. Gretzinger	$0.30
-	butter can	$0.05	Cramer	$0.05
6	egg crates	$0.30	M.H. Schrack	$0.25
-	-	-	H. Charles	$0.25
-	-	-	J.C. Tucker	$0.20
-	-	-	J.C. Ohler	$0.15
-	-	-	Norris	$0.10
4	sap pails	$0.20	Wm. Gregg	$0.10
1	sack flour	$0.25	Geo. Anderson	$0.10
-	flour in box	$0.50	Cramer	$0.35

1	scale	$8.00	Mrs. Herring	$12.00
1	lb oats	$0.25	Geor. Yates	$0.30
1	lb "	$0.25	G.W. Berry	$0.25
1	hopper wheat	$0.65	Geor. Yates	$0.70
1	box scraps	$0.05	H. Rummel	$0.15
1	gal measure	$0.10	C. Gretzinger	$0.11
1	cold chisel & punch	$0.05	J. Ohler	$0.15
1	bit & cold chisel	$0.05	-	-
3	wrenches	$0.05	S. McDermott	$0.40
1	sieve & scoop	$0.10	Allie Berry	$0.06
1	peck & ½ p measure	$0.25	Wm. Gregg	$0.20
1	white p.k. measure	$0.05	S. McKonkie	$0.20 total
½	bu corn	$0.25	"	-
3	bu mixed feed	$0.50	Gregg	$0.35
6	grain sacks 10¢	$0.60	Hunter	$2.30 total
6	do	$0.60	"	-
6	do	$0.60	"	-

Page 13

No. of Items	Description as Inventoried	Value	To Whom Sold	Price
6	do	$0.60	" [Hunter]	-
1	bu basket	$0.10	B. Berry	$0.05
1	corn sheller	$1.00	J.C. Tucker	$2.50
1	pile oak boards	$1.00	Land Snyder	$1.00

6½ doz	buckets 50¢	$3.25	L. Snyder	$4.68
1	basket	$0.20	D. Zody	$0.51
1	meat saw	$0.25	O.A. Mitchell	$0.50
2	sheep skins & b	$0.25	D. Zody	$0.51 total
1	box scoop & twine	$0.05	"	-
1	new jar	$0.05	"	-
1	coal stove & pipe	$1.50	E.A. Moffitt	$0.75
1	jug oil	$0.05	Gretzinger	$0.05
1	hoe	$0.10	J.C. Tucker	$0.15
1¼	bu onions	$0.40	M. Pitts	$0.50
20	bu potatoes 10¢	$2.00	Ezra Snyder	$3.33 total
7	bu "	10¢	$0.70	"
1	grind stone	$0.25	J. Tucker	$1.00
1	calf rack & sled	$0.05	S. McKonkie	$0.10
1	1 horse wagon	$2.00	C. Gretzinger	$2.25
1	1 horse spring w.	$0.50	S. McKonkie	$1.25
1	double shovel plow	$0.25	M.H. Schrack	$0.20
1	single " "	$0.25	McDermott	$0.25
1	harrow	$1.00	D. Zody	$4.70
1	2 horse wagon	$5.00	Wm. Gregg	$8.00
1	cow	$22.00	T.J. Wilson	$28.00
5	hogs	$25.00	N. Moury	$30.50

Page 14

No. of Items	Description as Inventoried	Value	To Whom Sold	Price
34	fence posts/5¢	$1.70	J. Marks	$1.70
2	scantling	$0.10	J. Hunter	$0.18
2	rakes & scrap iron	$0.05	J Tucker	$0.15

Total value of goods $201.85
Amount of money + $9.19
$211.04

Total sale income: $309.31

SELECTED BIBLIOGRAPHY

Books

Baughman, A.J. *A Centennial History of Richland County, Ohio*. Chicago: A.T. Andreas, 1873.

Bratton, Daniel, ed. *Yrs. Ever Affly: The Correspondence of Edith Wharton and Louis Bromfield*. East Lansing: Michigan State University Press, 2000.

Bromfield, Louis. *Pleasant Valley*. New York: Harper & Brothers Publishers, 1945.

Graham, A.A. *History of Richland County*. Mansfield, OH: A.A. Graham & Company, 1880.

Heyman, Stephen. *The Planter of Modern Life: Louis Bromfield and the Seeds of a Food Revolution*. New York: W.W. Norton & Company, 2020.

History of Lower Scioto Valley, Ohio. Chicago: Inter-State Publishing Company, 1884.

Mitchell, Brett J. *Triple Murder: The Crimes Committed by Celia Rose*. Jeromesville, OH: HistoricalPreservation.org Press, 2007.

Schrack, Flora. *The Dream Mill: Poems for Children*. Los Angeles, CA: Walton & Wright Publishers, 1941.

Scott, Ivan. *Louis Bromfield, Novelist and Agrarian Reformer: The Forgotten Author* Lampeter, Ceredigion, Wales: Edwin Mellen Press Limited, 1998.

Woodyard, Chris. *Haunted Ohio*. Beavercreek, OH: Kestrel Publications, 1991.

Periodicals, Miscellaneous Articles and Other Media

Butler Daily Enterprise. "Criminal Cases." September 10, 1896, 7.

————. "Family Was Undoubtedly Poisoned with Arsenic." July 9, 1896, 4.

Butler Enterprise. "Celia Rose Mentally Defective." September 17, 1896, 7.

————. "Celia Rose Trial." October 8, 1896, 7.

————. "Grand Jury Indictments." September 24, 1896, 3.

Chicago Tribune. "Awful Peril of a Girl." August 17, 1896, 2.

Cleveland Journal of Medicine 6. "Medical News" (1901).

Columbus Medical Journal: A Magazine of Medicine and Surgery 17. "News Notes and Personals" (1897).

Grimm, Tim. "Celia Rose." *The Back Fields*. Wind River Records, 2005.

Heier, Angeline Schrack. "My Childhood Memories of the Rose Family." Unpublished document. Malabar Farm State Park Archives, date unknown, circa 1976.

Lee, Virginia. "Triple Rose Slayings Here 52 Years Ago." *Mansfield News Journal*, September 12, 1948.

Mansfield Daily Shield. "Family Poisoned." July 1, 1896, 4.

————. "Grave Suspicions." July 2, 1896, 4.

————. "No Doubt of It." July 11, 1896, 5.

————. "Post Mortem Examination." July 6, 1896, 6.

————. "Walter Rose Dead." July 5, 1896, 5.

————. "Witnesses Examined." July 9, 1896, 5.

Mansfield News. "McCombs [Obituary]." September 2, 1902.

Mansfield News Journal. "Richland's Patients." December 14, 1900, 5.

————. "State Parks Not Immune to Ghosts." October 31, 1982.

Richland Shield and Banner. "Newville [Neighborhood News]." June 27, 1896, 10.

————. "Third Death, The." July 21, 1896, 4.

————. "Third Victim." July 25, 1896, 3.

Saturday Globe (Utica, NY). "Poisoned Her Family." August 29, 1896, 1.

Schrack, Flora. "Triple Murder in Pleasant Valley." *Columbus Dispatch Magazine* (November 29, 1970).

Semi-Weekly News. "Another Victim." July 7, 1896, 6.

————. "Was It Poison." July 3, 1896, 7.

Wandering Appalachia blog. "The Mysterious Murders of John Newman and Louise Doyle." April 16, 2021. wanderingappalachia.org.

Interviews

Berry, Robert, Loudonville, Ohio. Interviewed at Malabar Farm State Park, Lucas, Ohio, 2004 and 2015.

Bowsher, James R., Wapakoneta, Ohio. Interviewed at the Temple of Tolerance, Wapakoneta, Ohio, and at Malabar Farm State Park, Lucas, Ohio, 2004, 2007, 2008, 2012 and 2020.

Reed, James, Lucas, Ohio. Interviewed at Malabar Farm State Park, Lucas, Ohio, 2004 and 2015.

Smith, Joe, Millersport, Ohio. Interviewed at Malabar Farm State Park, Lucas, Ohio, 2014 and 2015.

INDEX

Richland County, Ohio 9, 31, 38, 147, 148

Roos, Wilhelm 21

Rose, Celia F. 9, 10, 11, 12, 18, 20, 30, 44, 45, 50, 54, 55, 56, 57, 58, 63, 64, 65, 66, 68, 69, 72, 74, 80, 82, 83, 84, 88, 89, 90, 91, 92, 93, 94, 95, 96, 99, 100, 101, 102, 103, 104, 105, 106, 107, 108, 109, 110, 111, 112, 113, 114, 115, 116, 117, 118, 119, 120, 121, 122, 125, 126, 130, 133, 136, 137, 139, 140, 141, 142, 143, 144, 147

alleged sexual perversion of 111, 113

developmental disability of 44, 53, 71, 94

locket belonging to 22, 125, 126, 128

Rose, David S. 17, 18, 19, 21, 23, 26, 28, 29, 35, 43, 48, 49, 53, 59, 60, 62, 77, 87, 94, 95, 96, 97, 98, 99, 100, 105, 110, 117, 118, 128, 129

Rose, Julia Ann 26, 30, 31, 32, 35, 37, 43

Rose, Lawrence 21, 26

Rose, Virgil D. 105

Rose, Walter W. 17, 19, 20, 26, 31, 35, 43, 47, 48, 51, 54, 56, 59, 60, 61, 62, 65, 67, 68, 69, 77, 81, 86, 90, 95, 96, 98, 99, 103, 122

sexuality of 44

Ross County, Ohio 31, 37, 120, 121

Rough-on-Rats 56, 78, 89, 91, 96, 99

S

Saturday Globe 86

Schoharie County, New York 21

Schrack, Charles 33, 38, 42, 51

Schrack, David 34, 38

Schrack, Flora 10, 47, 48, 49, 68, 105, 145

Schrack, Marion 102, 108

Schrack, Maud 107

Schrack Mill 17, 33, 34, 35, 42, 136

Serpent Mound 22

Setty, James B. 119

Shawshank Redemption, The 9

Shoemaker Creek 23

Sinking Spring, Ohio 21, 23, 26

Sixty-Third Regiment, Ohio Volunteer Infantry 26, 28, 29, 35

smear case 66, 78, 85, 97, 106

Smith, Joe 41

Smith, Vilma (pseudonym) 135

South Salem, Ohio 119

Spenzer, Dr. John 92, 97, 100, 102, 103, 107

Stultz, Margaret 22

Sunfish Creek 23

Switzer's Run 17, 19, 34, 40, 48, 51, 53

T

Tallmadge, Ohio 54

Toledo State Hospital 114, 115, 120, 121, 122

Triple Murder: The Crimes Committed by Celia Rose 141

Tucker, Aurelius 106

Tucker, Eva 45, 101

V

Valley Hall School 9, 18, 38, 44, 45, 65, 73, 76, 95, 101, 102, 106, 112

W

Wapakoneta, Ohio 122

weaving 17, 18, 44, 48

Welty, Christian 33, 42

Wise, Phoebe 63, 132, 140

Wolfe, Judge Norman 94, 96, 109, 112, 114

Woodyard, Chris 12, 137

Worden, Lucretia 21

ABOUT THE AUTHOR

MARK SEBASTIAN JORDAN is an award-winning playwright, poet, music critic, historian and storyteller who lives near Loudonville in Appalachian Ohio. He has received awards from the Ohio Arts Council, the Ohio Poetry Association, the Associated Press, the Richland County Foundation and the Ohio Theatre Alliance, as well as received the Jesse Stuart Memorial Award, the Gerald B. Rice Theater Award, the Florence B. Allen Literary Award, the Case Reserve Review Award and others.

He has been seen on such television programs as *Ghost Hunters*, *Mysteries at the Museum*, *My Ghost Story* and *House of the Unknown*. He was also an extra in the classic film *The Shawshank Redemption* and today often tells stories about it at the historic Ohio State Reformatory in Mansfield, Ohio, where the movie was filmed. He writes a weekly local history column, "History Knox," for KnoxPages.com and has performed extensively throughout Ohio as a storyteller, living history reenactor and poet. He is program annotator and pre-concert speaker for the Mansfield Symphony and writes music reviews of the Cleveland Orchestra, Apollo's Fire, the Boston Symphony and more for *Seen & Heard International* and *MusicWeb International*.

His previous works include:

A Drunk in the Night (produced in 1994 by the Theta Alpha Phi Drama Honor Fraternity)

Burnin' Love (produced in 1995 by the Theta Alpha Phi Drama Honor Fraternity)

The Comedy of Eros (cowritten with Bryan Gladden; produced in 1996 by the Theta Alpha Phi Drama Honor Fraternity)

Awaiting (translation of original German monodrama *Erwartung* by Marie Pappenheim; produced in 1997 by the Theta Alpha Phi Drama Honor Fraternity)

Theater Monologues: "The Director," "The Critic," "Nothing but Light" and "Stages" (produced in 1998 by the Theta Alpha Phi Drama Honor Fraternity)

Swan Dive (produced in 1999 by the Theta Alpha Phi Drama Honor Fraternity)

Ceely (produced in 2003–4, 2007–8 and 2012 by Mansfield Playhouse/Malabar Farm Foundation)

Phoebe (produced in 2005–6 by Mansfield Playhouse/Malabar Farm Foundation)

Phoebe: The Script (Sinister Hand Media, 2006)

Bicentennial Chautauqua: George Hawkins (Produced by the Mansfield Centennial Commission, 2008)

The Book of Jobs (Pudding House Press, 2010)

1776 & All That (XOXOX Press, 2010)

Louie (produced in 2010 and 2011 by Mansfield Playhouse/Malabar Farm Foundation)

Murder Ballads (Poets Haven Press, 2014)

The Ghost of Ceely Rose (produced in 2015 by the Malabar Farm Foundation)

The World (produced in 2016 by The Alchemists)

i am carlos (produced in 2016 by The Alchemists)

Slammer, Private Dick (Sinister Hand Media, 2017)

His living history presentations include:
Hallelujah: The Glory and Fury of George Frideric Handel
Copperhead: Clement Vallandigham
The Man Behind the Curtain: Louis Bromfield's Secretary, George Hawkins
This Is Orson Welles (Parts I and II)